My Dad John

Learning Life's Lessons from Dad

Ray Hackert

ISBN 978-1-62806-352-3   (print | paperback)

Library of Congress Control Number 2022912259

Published by
Salt Water Media
29 Broad Street, Suite 104
Berlin, MD 21811
www.saltwatermedia.com

Salt Water
MEDIA

Dedication

To the memory of my dad, John Paul Hackert

Acknowledgements

Thanks to my daughter Margaret. She was the primary editor. By writing this book, she was learning with me how to write and publish a book, which turned out to be a very interesting activity.

In addition, thanks to my daughter Janet, who could bring into this book her job background and experience with writing and publishing pamphlets and radio talks, for example.

Table of Contents

PART 3

Introduction

This book is a collection of my memories of my dad, John Paul Hackert. It includes stories about my dad and stories my dad told me which I've heard throughout my life. It is supported by the Hackert family tree and records provided by Sister Venard (Lucy, my dad John's youngest sister), who first collected them in about 1940. The information was then handed on to and updated by John's sister Bernice, followed by my cousin Leon Spors, and now in 2019, my niece Elizabeth (Betsy) Hackert Gertonson Howe.

It also contains some of the learnings and skills I've gotten from my dad. Various people in the family have asked me to tell them about my dad, so this is my story of Dad.

How the Book Is Arranged

In Part 1, Chapters 1 through 14, the book covers the story of my dad John's ancestors, his birth, life as a child, teenager, and adult, and his death at age 89½. Some of the chapters will take you through his marriage, working at two careers, and retirement.

In Part 2, chapters 15 through 26, various aspects of John's life are covered, such as John the hunter, John the miller, and John the butcher.

Part 3 of this book contains family pictures and comments, including people, houses, and documents.

Places in
My Dad John

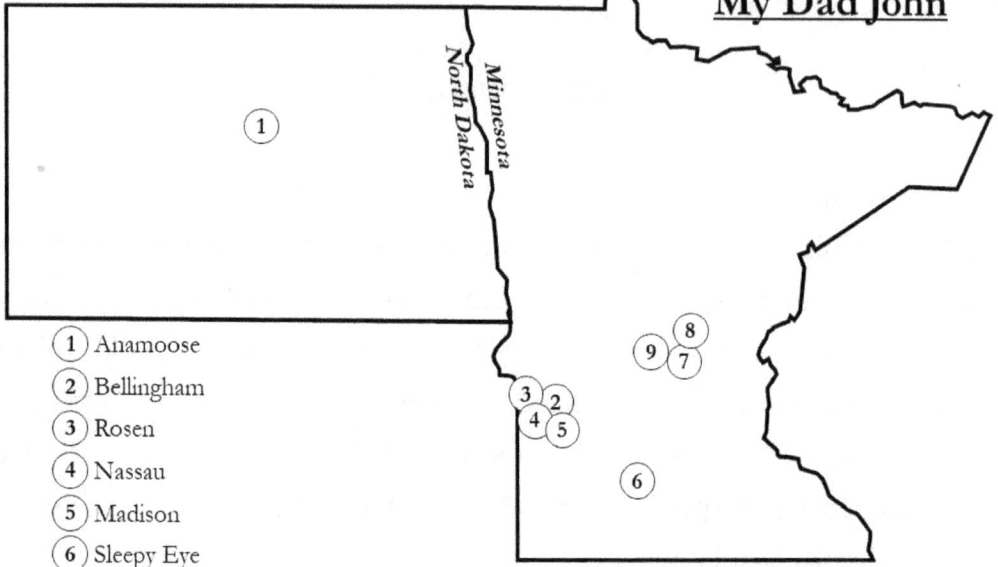

(1) Anamoose
(2) Bellingham
(3) Rosen
(4) Nassau
(5) Madison
(6) Sleepy Eye
(7) St. Cloud
(8) Mayhew Lake
(9) St. John's University (Collegeville)

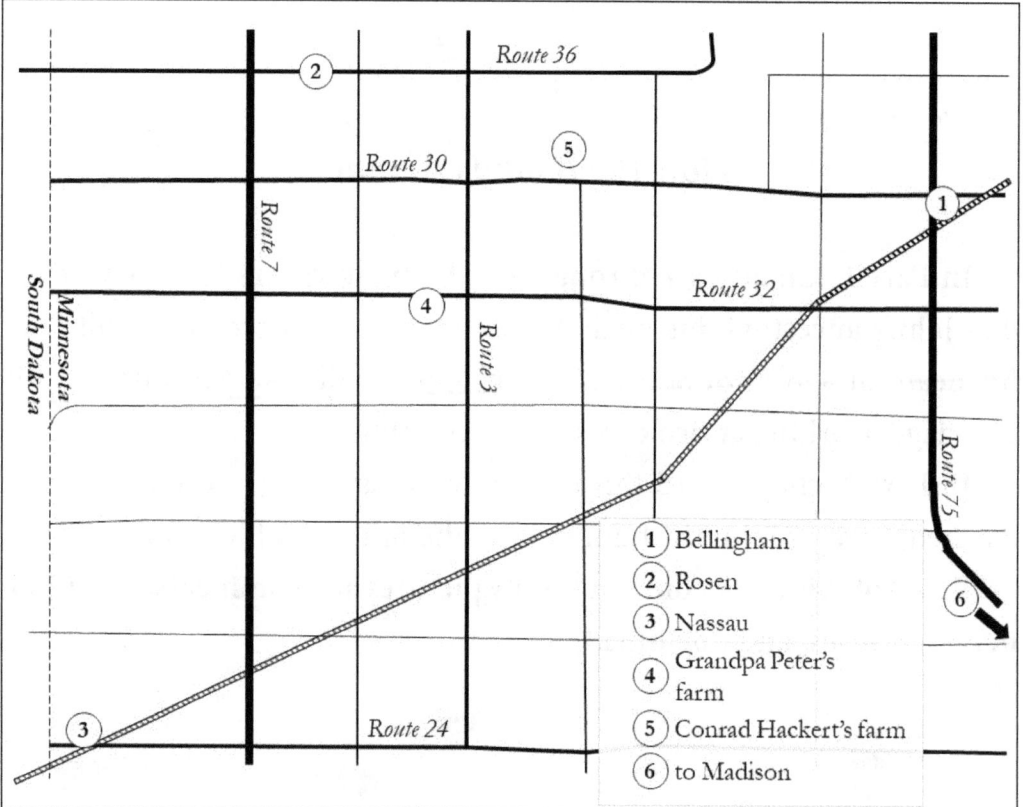

Minnesota
North Dakota

Route 36

Route 30

Route 7

Route 32

Route 3

Minnesota
South Dakota

Route 75

Route 24

(1) Bellingham
(2) Rosen
(3) Nassau
(4) Grandpa Peter's farm
(5) Conrad Hackert's farm
(6) to Madison

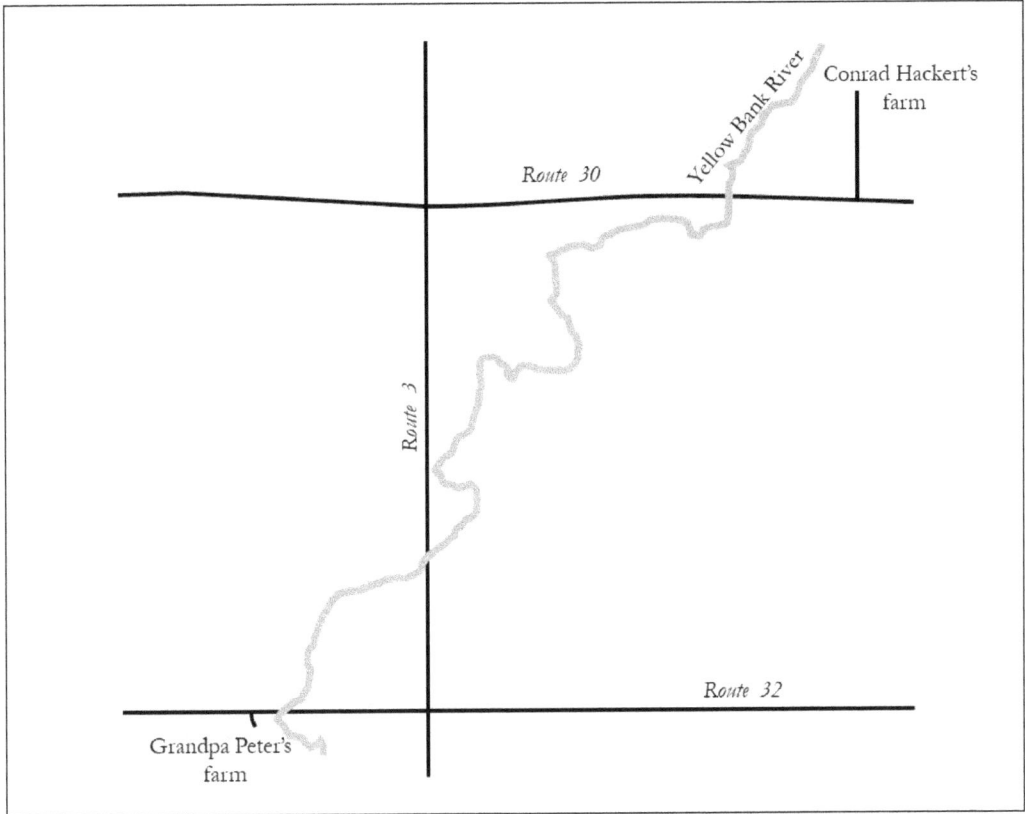

Route 30

Yellow Bank River

Conrad Hackert's farm

Route 3

Route 32

Grandpa Peter's farm

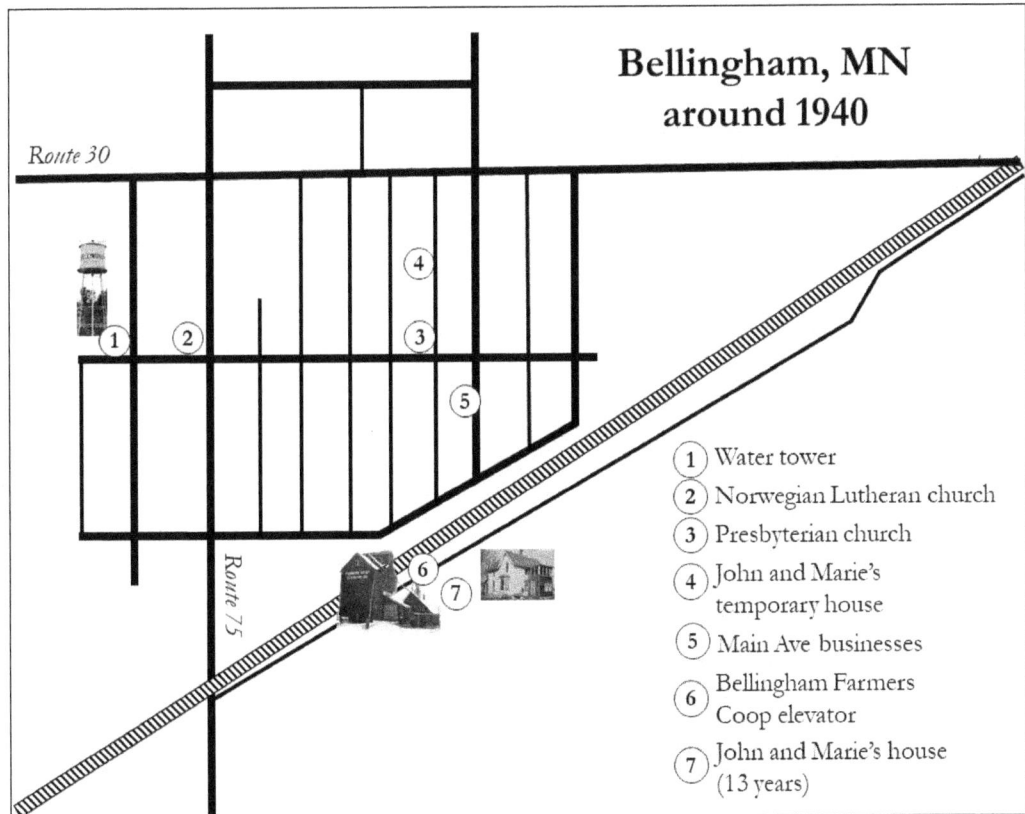

Bellingham, MN around 1940

Route 30

Route 75

1 Water tower
2 Norwegian Lutheran church
3 Presbyterian church
4 John and Marie's temporary house
5 Main Ave businesses
6 Bellingham Farmers Coop elevator
7 John and Marie's house (13 years)

PART 1

The Events

in the

Life of My Dad

Chapter 1

John's Ancestors – 1700s to 1881

"…And it came to pass, in those days…" It was after 1750, when the end of the Little Ice Age meant that the Northern Hemisphere was warming up. With longer, warmer summers, it became easier to grow more food. As a result, more people began to populate what is now Europe. Eventually there were more people than food supplies, particularly in periods of low rainfall, and starvation would come upon the population.

One of the stories handed down by word-of-mouth in my family was an example of these hard times. One evening, the family—a dad and mom (my great-grandparents) and four kids around 3 to 12 years old—had only six potatoes and milk (from their own cows) to eat. So the mother decided to make potato soup. Just as they were sitting down to eat, there was a knock on the door. The neighbor family with three kids had arrived, and they announced that they had nothing to eat. The family was invited in, and Great-Grandma added more water to the soup. They all ate quietly and then agreed it was a wonderful supper.

My story about my father begins in Europe in the early to middle 1800s. A guy by the name of Bismarck arrived on the scene and decided to consolidate the small kingdoms and fiefdoms into one large German nation. Amongst these groups lived my forefathers, the Hackert clan.

In those times, it was the custom that the oldest son would inherit the family farm (such as it was). The second son would be a priest, and the remaining sons would be drafted into Bismarck's army to fight to consolidate the German principalities. This did not sit well with my ancestors; why go off to war and get blown up or shot? They were intelligent people and wanted to do the rational thing for the welfare of themselves, their family, and their friends. So they decided to leave this warring country and go off to America, hopefully to achieve more freedom.

Apparently, my ancestors were fairly well off—certainly not poor. They excelled in farming, at least in good-weather times; they knew the building crafts using wood and stone, and had mechanical know-how. They also had good social skills—they got along with their neighbors and worked well with them. Even in those days, farming was a complex activity. One had to know what would grow in what kind of soil, the best plants to grow, how much fertilizer (manure) to use for each crop, when to plant, when and where to do soil cultivation, and the markets available for any surplus that was grown.

❧ *Chapter 2* ❧

The Hackerts Arrive in America

In 1881, Great-Grandpa Peter Hackert (Peter Sr.) collected all the family possessions, including farm tools, woodworking tools, building tools and equipment, and as much money as possible, and left Europe for the Lac qui Parle County and Bellingham, Minnesota area by way of New York City. They brought with them not only the family, but also two railroad cars full of their possessions to establish a new life in Minnesota.

Peter Hackert Sr., with wife and five kids—Albert, 14 years of age; Peter, 11; John, 8 (uncle to my dad John later in life); Rosalia, 4; and Agnes, the baby—arrived in Lac qui Parle County in Minnesota, in the area of Bellingham, Minnesota (incorporated later, in 1887). By 1883, Peter Sr. bought a 153-acre farm along the Yellow Bank River (which my family always called the Yellow Bank Creek) about 2 to 3 miles straight west of Bellingham. In later years, he bought a few more acres of land adjacent to his farm to complete the farm as I knew it in 1932 and on.

Grandpa Peter Sr.'s wife had died before leaving Europe in 1881, and he had remarried. They had several more children, including Conrad Hackert. When Peter Sr. died, the farm went to Conrad, who I got to know when I first lived in Minnesota. When he became an adult, Peter Sr.'s son, Peter Jr. (my Grandpa Peter) married Martha Semrau.

Chapter 3

Grandpa Peter Homesteads

At 27 years old, Grandpa Peter Jr. homesteaded 160 acres (a quarter section, meaning a quarter of a square mile) in Lac qui Parle County, about 6 miles west of Bellingham along the Yellow Bank River. That is about 2 miles from his father's farm that was later held by Peter Sr.'s son Conrad. This 160-acre parcel was customarily the size that one man could farm with horses, probably with some help, mainly at harvest time. Later on, Grandpa Peter Jr. bought a 40-acre parcel known as the "south forty."

Looking at the history of my family can be confusing because there were two John Hackerts—my dad John and Grandpa Peter's half-brother John. I never met that other John. He acquired the building later known in the family as the "John Hackert building" in Nassau, Minnesota. In later years, the John Hackert building was used by my uncle Alvin (called Pete) and Aunt Bernice as a grocery store; earlier, the basement was a bar and pool hall where Alvin worked. Beer sold at a nickel a glass there in 1947.

A key issue I heard about after growing up was that the family goal from the start in the USA was to learn fluent, commercial English. They knew from their European experience that one had to know the local language if one wanted to be successful in business. More than anything else, Great-Grandpa was a businessman from the start in the USA, a farmer and a craftsman. Without good knowledge of local languages, he would probably have been robbed blind and not even known it.

So Grandpa Peter set out to be an excellent farmer and craftsman, organizing his family farm to be mainly self-sufficient. He also had enough land to have a cash crop each year to aid in buying necessities such as farm machinery, pigs, cattle, and chickens to improve and modernize the farm, and to have a few luxuries.

One luxury was pipe tobacco. He grew it in Minnesota, even though the agronomists said it was impossible because of the climate. At least it was good enough for Grandpa. (I do not smoke, so I am not an authority on that.) I must say, though, that my dad and uncles and cousins bought their tobacco, maybe because they were well off enough, or because the younger generation is often not committed to doing what old Dad did. They smoked cigarettes, not pipes, and—early on—rolled their own, like one sees cowboys do in movies of the Old West.

When Great-Grandpa Peter and his family arrived in Minnesota in 1881, the second son, also named Peter, was 11 years old. This was the Grandpa Peter I knew when I was 5 years old. Grandpa Peter, along with his brothers and sisters, uncles and aunts, and cousins (by the dozens) are the generation I knew from early in my life.

Grandpa Peter married his first wife (Martha Semrau Hackert) and had five children: Frank, Mary, John (known as Hans from the German word for John, Johann, and known to me as Dad), Elizabeth, and Lucy (Sister Venard). Then this wife died, and he remarried. Grandpa Peter's second wife, Ida (Voigt), had four children: Wilbert, Bernice, and twins Alice and Alvin (known as Pete).

I believe my father had red hair. I never heard it said, but in my early youth (up to 5 years old), when he let his hair grow out somewhat, I recall that he had red sideburns. I also suspect that Dad's sister Lucy had red hair. Again, I never heard that, but I believe it. But I do not know for sure, because, as a conservative Benedictine nun, she always had her head covered. (I saw her near death with her head uncovered and her hair was grayish white.) Red hair is prevalent in the Hackert family. In my family, my daughter Joan had vivid red hair. Also, redheaded cousins ran in the Frank Hackert family and in the Mary Hackert Spors family.

My father, John, was probably born in the first house that was on the Hackert homestead. About 1915, a new house was built. My dad told us about how he, as a teenager, helped build the house using the family knowledge of woodworking and craftsmanship (framing, second floor supports, doors, windows, closets, rooms, roof construction, etc.). He told of hauling lumber with a team of horses and wagon for 6 miles from the Bellingham lumberyard to the farm. All this construction went on while they were planting and cultivating the fields and garden, and doing routine chores like milking, feeding the pigs and chickens, caring for the horses, and making hay for the cattle.

When I first saw the farm when I was 5 years old, there was a small house at the entrance to the driveway that, at most, had two or three rooms. I understood that it had been moved from where the new house was being built, out to the entrance of the driveway. Grandpa Peter, I believe, used that building then for his tools and woodworking.

Of course, all the construction took money. I never heard this, but my opinion from reading a number of books on economics, especially in the Midwest, is that the cash crop in those days was wheat, and that around 1914 wheat was 5 dollars a bushel. In a couple years, a farm family could very likely sell about 1000 bushels, amounting to about $5,000. At that time, with $2,000 or $3,000, one could build a nice multi-room house with a full upstairs, downstairs, and basement (cellar).

During the timeframe of building the house, Grandma Ida convinced Grandpa Peter to add a washhouse behind the main house for Grandma and their daughters to do the family laundry. Eventually, around the 1930s, Grandpa bought Grandma an electric washing machine. Their son Wilbert, who was a young man in those days, worked and played with electricity, and wired the house for electricity by hooking up a wind-powered generator to the windmill—which had been built to pump water for the farm. So their family had 35-volt electricity when most farmers just had kerosene lamps. (That was the latest thing, with Rockefeller and his kerosene business.) Later wind power was not enough, so Wilbert designed, bought components for, and built an electric generator which was placed in the basement, with exhaust exiting outside via a pipe through the foundation. After we moved to Bellingham and I was about 5 years old, I would stay over on a weekend and I would be awakened by the generator going on, maybe around 6 AM. It was Monday morning, Wash Day, and the generator was to run Grandma's washing machine.

Shortly after building the house, my dad John was assigned the task of building a smokehouse for meats, especially sausage, including blood sausages. When I was about 35 or 40 years old, my dad spent hours one day showing me around the farm, and particularly telling me about designing the smokehouse. He got advice from uncles and his dad, and read about how to get the smoke to stay and permeate the hanging meats, how to choose the correct kind of wood to get the best flavor to the meat, and how long to smoke it. The process was kind of like making good wine or bourbon. He also showed me and explained to me about the building of the barn and hog barn, and piping water to them for the animals. The barn was built on the side of a hill with a drive-in access to the haybarn. There was storage space for feed in the haybarn area, with chutes to deliver the feed to the cattle below.

The handling of hay was mechanized to move hay into the haybarn from a hayrack (hay wagon). The mechanism included two slings. Half the hay was loaded onto the bottom sling on the hayrack, and the rest onto the top sling. The hayrack would be driven into the hay barn. Each sling on the hayrack would be raised up on pulleys and rails suspended from the ceiling of the barn and moved to roughly where the hay should be placed. The sling release would be pulled by the operator and the hay would be dumped—no pitching hay by hand.

I haven't mentioned it so far, but in the earliest days after arriving at the "Hackert Homestead" in Minnesota, Grandpa Peter planted a grove of trees around the house to shelter it from northwest winter winds and snow. He included all sorts of fruit trees, mainly apples. They planted gardens around the grove and near the house, for all kinds of vegetables and greens such as lettuce to aid the family's self-sufficiency. For example, they grew enough potatoes for a year, enough apples for a year, and squash and pumpkins and carrots, all of which could be stored in the cool, non-freezing cellar for months. They also grew much cabbage and converted it to sauerkraut in big, maybe 20- or 40-gallon crocks. The sauerkraut kept for many months stored in open crocks in the cellar, since the acidity of the acetic acid kept it from spoiling.

Chapter 4

Young John

As a very young lad, John was especially inquisitive. As an example, when he was about 4 years old, he got to thinking about a saying he had heard in the family, "It is about as quick as fat through a goose." His mom raised geese, so they were around all the time. So one day, when Ma was cutting up pork chops for supper, he asked for and got a piece of pig fat, carved off a chop. He got ahold of a long piece of Ma's knitting yarn and tied it to the pork fat. Finally, the great experiment—he tossed the fat amongst Ma's tame geese feeding in the yard. Very quickly, a goose grabbed it and swallowed it. Soon it arrived out the other end of the goose. Of course, as it dropped to the ground, another hungry goose gobbled it up. Then another goose ate it, and another and another. Soon three or four or five geese were all strung together on his yarn, and were making a lot of noise. Hearing all the squawking, Ma came out to see what was upsetting her pride and joy, her flock of geese. John was chastised, but not very much, since his Pa thought his adventure showed John had a sharp mind.

Another memorable situation happened when John was probably about 9 or 10 years old. He was serving Mass on Sunday and Father Goersel was giving his sermon. After a while, Father noticed that John was not in his assigned seat, so he looked around and saw that John was sitting on Father's new motorcycle in the sacristy, playing like he was riding down the road at 50 miles an hour. Of course, that came to an abrupt stop. Father had recently bought the motorcycle to replace his horse, but wasn't ready to share it with a little boy.

Another story—when John was about 10 or 12 years old, he had saved up enough money, so he bought a 12-gauge shotgun, a Winchester

Model 1898 with slide-pump action for multiple repeating shots. John had been hunting on the far side of the Yellow Bank River from the house, and it was raining heavily. On the way home, the creek had risen so he could not easily wade across it. He decided to go downstream and cross at the bridge, but when he got there, water was flowing over it. He decided to wade across on the bridge, and fortunately he was not swept downstream.

In his early teens, John got a job to help rebuild that bridge—to build it higher and make it of steel. His job was to move dirt with a team of horses, pulling a sliding bucket to scoop up dirt and move it to the approaches of the bridge, so later the road could be built to cross on the higher bridge.

The road past their house was a township road. Township roads were typically around every square mile to connect the farmsteads on each quarter section—quarter of a square mile—of farmland. John was hired and paid by the township organization to use horses and a grader to maintain these gravel (sometimes dirt) roads.

By the time John was, say, 12 to 17 years old, he took his place, to the extent he could, in the family activities like plowing and planting, and chores such as milking and feeding the animals, cultivating the fields and gardens, trimming orchard trees, and fixing broken implements and machinery. And at about 16 or 17, he was one of a number of people who built the new house while keeping up with all the other jobs. It took a lot of work to keep the family self-sufficient, with Dad and Mom and nine children growing up.

My dad John told me a story where, when he was about 15 to 17, he went to a Halloween dance at the nearby hall in Rosen, costumes optional. Since, in those days, there was no TV or radio, one type of entertainment was to go to dances. He had been at the dance for about an hour when this little old lady in costume came in. She was an excellent dancer, very popular, and danced with many of the young bucks as well as others. At the end of the dance, they agreed that this little old lady got the prize for the best costume. Then each in costume had to come up and identify themselves. When the little old lady took off "her" mask, everyone saw a mustache and beard. The "little old lady" turned out to be John's dad, Grandpa Peter! Although I didn't completely believe it, I felt it was a good story.

In my early youth, I expected the story was embellished, but that was not so. In later years, before her death, I told that story to my Aunt Bernice, Dad's younger sister. She explained that when she was 8 years old, Grandpa Peter had waited until the others went off to the dance, and she had helped him find a wig, padding for his chest, and an old dress of Ma's (Grandma Ida), and got him into his costume. So I guess Grandpa Peter fooled them all! I imagine that all the young bucks that had danced with John's dad (as a woman) were quite embarrassed.

Chapter 5

The Marriage of John Hackert and Marie Schreder

DAD'S EARLY LIFE

My parents were born 4 months apart—my dad was born October 21, 1898, and my mom was born February 21, 1899. Both grew up on farms—John in Lac qui Parle County, near Bellingham, Minnesota, and Marie near Mayhew Lake, Minnesota, which even today is a crossroads village with a Catholic church. My dad and mom are buried there.

John went only to grade school, at a country school across the road from their farmhouse. My dad told me that for several years, summer school involved the kids learning High (classical) German so they could read and write it, so my dad was proficient in that.

My understanding is that High (classical) German is a "made" language, introduced by Bismarck when he consolidated the German principalities, since he wanted the Germans to use a language that all Germans could understand in their new German nation. This is not unusual. In Africa, the same sort of thing happened. In more recent years since World War II, the area of Africa including Kenya and Tanzania has a "made" language, Swahili. Just as in Germany there were many village languages, so to unify the people, Swahili was developed. Since this was in the area of German East Africa, there are German words incorporated into Swahili such as shule (school) and hela (money or coin).

When John was about 19 or 20 years old, he was chosen by Grandpa Peter to drive him and Grandma Ida, John's stepmother, to go visit the Voigt relatives. (Grandma Ida was a Voigt.) Eventually, they got to the home of Grandma Ida's cousin Ignatius Voigt, who lived on the farm near Mayhew Lake. As my dad John described it, they drove up to the farm, and he got out of the car with camera in hand. He noticed activity behind the house, so he walked back there. He came across this beautiful young lady in old clothes—apron on, hair up in a bun—scrubbing laundry on a scrubbing board in a tub of wash water. Of course, even before being introduced, he took her picture—he showed it to me often in my youth. They wrote back and forth for a limited time, saw each other several times, and married in June 1921 when both were 22. I assume each was smitten by the other from the beginning.

Mother Marie's Early Life

The story of my dad John is not complete without describing the early life of his wife, Marie. After all, they married in 1921 and lived together until 1989—67 years as man and wife.

My mother's name when she was born was Mary, the same as her mother's. When she was very little, she was called "Little Mary," and she did not like that, so she demanded that people call her Marie. The name stuck and became hers for the rest of her life.

When my mother was about 8 or 10 years old, there was a crisis in the family (probably her dad being sick), and in the middle of the night, she was sent to get help from her uncle who lived about a mile away. She was carrying a kerosene lantern and made her way through the woods. She explained how she was expecting at any moment to be eaten by a bear, crashing out of the dark woods.

In my mother's early life, she was the oldest of 12 children on a farm near Mayhew Lake, Minnesota, about 12 miles outside St. Cloud and about 1 to 2 miles off the present US Highway 10. Steven Schreder, her dad, died in 1914, when Marie was about 14 years old. Being the oldest, during her dad's last days and after he died, she was very much involved with milking the cows, feeding the pigs, hauling hay, and doing other farm chores. Mom told me that the second oldest child, a sister named Anna, complained one day that she had to help with house chores and look after the younger kids (ten of them), and that Marie had the easy part. So they swapped jobs for a day and that settled it—Marie was the outside worker. Soon the Steven Schreder family acquired a hired man, Ignatius Voigt, to do the farming—planting and other chores. Not too long after that, her mother, Mary, and Ignatius married.

Marie's education was spotty through the 8th grade. There were always things at home to help with. But, for example, off and on, she would stay with Grandpa and Grandma Tinschert (Marie's mother's first in-laws) for a period of time to attend school. Then back home she would go, to help with the family.

As long as I knew my mother, she was an avid reader, so she knew a lot about many things, and encouraged us kids to read a lot. Growing up, we always had the town paper, the Minneapolis paper, and magazines like *Reader's Digest* and *Catholic Digest*. Wherever we lived, we used the local library and its books. When Marie was in her middle teens, the family decided the younger ones should go to Catholic school. Her parents put Marie in charge, and they rented an apartment in St. Cloud so the younger ones could go to school. Imagine Marie having the responsibility of buying groceries, doing laundry, and cooking for that tribe of younger brothers and sisters. Imagine members of the family traveling back and forth from the farm about 12 miles away in the time of traveling by horses and wagons.

At about the age of 19, Marie went off to Minneapolis to take a job as a maid in a "rich" family's home. She did well and saved her money toward her goal of a good marriage. As described elsewhere, she was at home on the farm doing the family washing when John came upon the scene. Her life was changed immediately.

After the Wedding and John's New Job

After their marriage, John and Marie went to live at the Hackert "homestead" and John remained the chief farmer for about 6 months.

16

Grandpa Peter was getting on in years, and was expected to retire to town with the family, and John and Marie would run the farm. My mother told me that was her expectation when they married, but that was not to happen. In retrospect, Grandma Ida wanted the next son in the family, Wilbert, the first child of Grandpa Peter and Ida, to farm with Peter, and later Peter and Ida would retire to town. Wilbert would eventually inherit the farm. (Peter was 51 in 1921, and he probably had another few years to continue. So he would work the farm with Wilbert for another decade and then retire, with Wilbert taking over at age 21.)

This was fine with John—although a well-trained farmer, by now he was not very interested in farming. About that time, the manager's job at the Farmers' Elevator Company of Bellingham (later renamed the Farmers Cooperative Elevator Company of Bellingham) became vacant and John got the job. That was a good fit since Edwin Hackert, Grandpa Peter's half-brother, managed the Peavey Elevator about a block away from the Farmers Elevator, and was available to teach Dad all about managing an elevator. According to my mother, during the first year or two Uncle Edwin spent many evenings talking, and Dad learning, all about the grain business.

When John and Marie moved to Bellingham so John could start the new job, they had a house either next door to or the second house north of the Norwegian Lutheran Church, which is a block down the hill from where the town water tower stands. The house is on the north side of the church and on the west side of US 75, which runs through Bellingham. While living in that house, their son Ralph was born in 1922 and Gerard in 1923.

During this period, 1921 and on, John's brother Frank had finished college and got a job at the bank in Bellingham. Together, the two brothers acquired a car. It was an Overland sedan with a fabric top and side curtains. The rule was that the car was John's one weekend and Frank's the next weekend. Of course, both went to church together in Rosen, 6 miles away. Dad showed me pictures of the car when I was a kid. I am sure, particularly in winter, one had to be bundled up in 10 to 20 degrees below zero weather.

Later, in 1926, Frank met and married a schoolteacher from Bellingham named Ruby Nelson.

Chapter 6

New Job in North Dakota – 1924 to 1932

Eventually, in 1924, Dad and the family moved to Anamoose, North Dakota. In Bellingham, my dad had grown tired of always being "Peter Hackert's son," and I am sure he got an increase in pay to move. Also, he knew Bill Nitz, a wheat farmer in Anamoose, who may have been on the elevator board of directors and could bring the news of a job opening in North Dakota to Dad. Bill Nitz was a relative of the Spors family, and Jack Spors was married to John's sister Mary.

Don (Donald) was born in North Dakota in 1925; I was born in 1927, Katie (Kathryn) was born in 1928, and Gerry (Geraldine) was born in 1930. We continued to live in North Dakota until 1932. (A section in Part 2 of this book covers "Memories of North Dakota" by a 5-year-old, Ray.) While we were in North Dakota, the drought brought hard times for farmers, and the board of directors voted to reduce Dad's pay even though he had been keeping the business profitable. Also at that time, the board of directors was recruiting Dad to come back to Bellingham to get the elevator out of accumulated debt. They even agreed to a bonus for him if this debt was gone in 10 years. He never met that goal, but was only a few hundred dollars short of qualifying for the bonus.

❧ *Chapter 7* ❧

We Move Back to Bellingham – 1932 to 1945

During the 1930s, the area around Bellingham suffered a terrible drought and unimaginably low grain prices—the worst conditions were around 1934. The United States was experiencing the Great Economic Depression throughout the 1930s.

In 1932, when we first moved to Bellingham from North Dakota, we lived near the middle of town. I was only about 5 years old, but I went to the store for Mom since it was only three blocks away. In that period of time, my mom had me buying and eating a cake of yeast each day—yeast such as one uses for making bread. I have no idea what that was for. Also, our well near the house was not good for drinking. That water was used for our cow and for laundry. I used my wagon and buckets to get drinking water from a house about a block and a half away. Along the side of the driveway was a small building that housed our cream separator. Extra milk was separated, and the cream was sold to the creamery in town which made Land O'Lakes butter.

Later, in August 1932, another kid was born in the John Hackert family. Her name was Lucille (and she was later called Rusty). This was my first memory of my mother birthing a kid. Mom hollered and carried on for a while until the baby arrived.

In the fall of that year, my dad and mom found a better place to rent and live. It was 5 acres, across the road from the elevator. Dad could walk to work in a few minutes. Before we moved in, since Mom disliked the color of the inside, she was repainting it. Mom brought us kids along, with Lucille in a buggy. Lucille was not a happy girl, and when Lucille hollered or cried, I was supposed to rock her to quiet her. So I was busy.

I would have preferred to investigate all the parts of the house, barn, and sheds, though. The inside of the house got painted and we moved in.

In 1934, when I was in first grade and my older brother Don was in the third grade, we attended Catholic grade school in Rosen. About the time we were getting ready to go home one day, Don fell on the basement stairs and cut his forehead. There was much bleeding. My dad came and took us to Madison to the doctor. We were having a dust storm that was bad enough so one could only see about three to five car lengths ahead. This was just like the Dust Bowl in *The Grapes of Wrath*, the movie of the Okies leaving Oklahoma for California during the Great Depression. Yes, Don's injury was fixed—no more problems.

❖ Chapter 8 ❖

Farmers Elevator in Bellingham

RUNNING THE ELEVATOR

My dad was very innovative at keeping the business profitable, just as he was in North Dakota. Besides buying and selling grain, Dad also sold coal, twine, and specialty feed in sacks as he did in North Dakota. Also, the Farmers Elevator in Bellingham had a milling operation, so farmers could formulate and have the grain ground as needed for chickens, pigs, and cattle.

One year, there was a wet corn crop from an early frost and early snow. Instead of letting this be a loss for the farmers and the elevator, he worked with Ray Baker, a trucker with a grain dealer license. They arranged that Dad would buy limited amounts of wet corn and sell it to Baker to deliver to turkey growers around Wilmar, Minnesota, to finish out turkeys for Thanksgiving and Christmas—a win-win for everybody.

Of course, the farmers had a way to fix the problem of wet corn. They would husk the corn and store it, hopefully until it dried, in a corncrib. This is a building that usually had wood slat sides or wire, so the corn would dry in several months from wind moving through the corn on cobs in the crib. After my dad's time, elevators got drying equipment for drying wet corn.

Another year, Dad also saw a way to make a profit with dockage, or weed seeds, accidentally included in grain. When wheat came in with buckwheat dockage one summer, he separated the buckwheat with a grain cleaner the elevator had for that purpose, and sold several railroad cars of the buckwheat for a premium. In another innovation, he checked the barley being brought in at threshing time, and found out that

22

some customers were delivering malting barley. He segregated it and sold several railroad cars to beer companies for a premium. He always worked with the grain buyers in Minneapolis to get the best dollar for the farmers' grain, and returned the premium to each individual farmer according to what they delivered, providing a good result for everyone in the co-op system. It was more work for Dad this way, but that was what he was being paid for.

HAY – 1934

Under my dad's management, the elevator served the community in another way. Around 1933-1934, Minnesota had a bad drought and dust storm period. Since the farmers could not grow enough feed for their animals, the government had a program to buy and deliver hay to the elevator. During that period, day after day, there would be long lines waiting at the elevator for each farmer to get hay. This involved getting the tare or empty weight of the farmer's wagon—usually a horse-drawn wagon, but occasionally a truck or a car with a trailer. Then they would load up with hay and return to get weighed again to determine the net weight of the hay. I do not know if any money exchanged hands between the farmer and the elevator for this service—I was only about 7 years old!

DAD'S DAY AT THE ELEVATOR

Typically, in Bellingham, Dad would come home from the elevator for lunch from about noon to 12:30. He would eat a quick lunch Mom had ready, then lie down on the parlor carpet, flat on his back, and nap for about 15 minutes—then he was off to work again. On Sunday, it was Mass in the morning, then Sunday dinner, then often he would have a 2-hour nap.

If work permitted, Dad would go pick up the mail at the post office, about three or four blocks away, later in the afternoon. There was no mail delivery—the train brought the mail to town between 1 PM and

3 PM. Then the post office people sorted it and placed it in post office boxes. It was also delivered to farmers by rural mail carriers.

In the elevator, my dad worked 6 days a week, 8 AM to 6 PM, and if busy, beyond 6 PM in times like threshing, and in the fall during corn harvest. If needed, Dad would hire extra help. Since he was mostly the only worker at the elevator, he did the books and accounting in the evening if necessary. It was a long workday, but thank God he had a regular job through the Depression years. He was innovative enough to make a regular profit that was divided among the co-op members he worked for and with.

MAKING A PROFIT IN HARD (AND GOOD) TIMES

I was in grade school in these Depression years (1930-1939), and many people were without jobs. To make matters worse, during that time, we had a drought; it's a wonder my dad was able to manage an elevator and make a profit at it with hardly any farmers getting any marketable harvests for several years. In our area, West Central Minnesota, for several years and especially during 1934, we had many bad dust storms like those portrayed in *The Grapes of Wrath*.

Many years later, I visited two elevator managers—Curt in Minnesota and Cathy in Nebraska. My question to each was that since corn, a major grain for each, had recently dropped from $7 a bushel to about $3.20 a bushel, did they lose a lot of money? In both cases, each explained that their business involved both buying and selling grain. On most days, they kept track and usually came out about even, no losses, whether a grain went down or up. This is what my dad practiced in the grain business: Just try to make a conservative profit by setting his buying price and selling price to cover a reasonable profit, including costs like electricity to move the grain, labor, taxes, and deterioration of the machinery. After all, any profit left over after running the business in a co-op went to the people who dealt with the co-op on a proportional basis. I have tried to make this idea clear with the examples I have given—the buckwheat dockage in wheat and the wet corn.

Dad Home Alone

During those times in summer while I was in grade school, we would go visit Mom's folks in St. Cloud for a week, and Dad would stay home alone. My dad John was not a cook. For example, when we came home from St. Cloud, all the dishes he had used were dirty. It looked as though he ate Post Toasties for all his meals, since bowls and spoons were all over the kitchen.

My dad's idea of a meal was meat, potatoes, bread, and a dessert like canned apricot sauce my mother had made. My dad, coming from a subsistence farm—Grandpa Peter's, mostly raised us that way. For example, my mother always had homemade bread and baked things like pies for the family, to stretch my dad's salary. Very occasionally we would have some store-bought stuff.

Norwegian vs. Low German

On Sunday afternoons, we would listen to our radio. (We didn't do much on Sunday. Dad worked 6 days a week, for cat's sake!) One Sunday, Dad listened to a Norwegian Lutheran church sermon on the radio, in the Norwegian language. My dad said Norwegian was so close to Low German that he could understand it. He had a lot of customers who were Norwegian, and he could communicate with them.

Renovating the Elevator

In the late 1930s, Dad guided the business to modernize the plant. This included fixing up the elevator siding, repainting, rebuilding the driveway, adding a new scale that could take the biggest trucks and loads, and installing a new steel pit with associated grain handling equipment.

For example, in Bellingham, next to the elevator was a derrick for loading granite that was trucked there from granite quarries in the Minnesota River bottom, about 6 miles away. Granite was loaded onto railroad flatcars and shipped to St. Cloud Finishing Sheds. Occasionally, Minnesota state police would pull over an "overloaded" granite truck—a semi-tractor and flatbed trailer—and it was run onto the new scale, which had much more capacity than a load of granite. Toward the end of John's period of elevator management in 1945, the largest grain trucks could be weighed and loaded with the new equipment.

I was about 10 years old during this period of renovating the elevator, and on a summer evening when repair work stopped, we kids could go hand-over-hand way up the scaffolding ropes to nearly the top of the elevator; I often wondered if Mom or Dad knew about that.

RAY AND THE GRAIN BUSINESS

The best way to really learn a business is from your dad, particularly if he is a good businessman—so I did.

Dad taught me about the grain business, which I worked at his discretion at times: I moved the railroad cars with a hand jack and spotted them—got them in just the right spot—for loading at the elevator; moved grain doors, which had multi-layered boards to cover the doorways of standard railroad cars; cleaned up dust around the milling area; cleaned up spilled grain out on the railroad track—and sold it to my dad; cut weeds around the elevator property; killed rats around the elevator; cleaned up trash; shoveled and swept out flat-bottomed bins to change from one grain to another; and helped and advised hired help when Dad had to go to a funeral or a business meeting.

Dad hung serious responsibility on me when it seemed the thing to do. When I was about 17, I was left in charge since Dad had to go to an important family funeral for a day or two. He told me that if we got in enough flax to fill a flax bin, I should call the company we dealt with in

Minneapolis to buy a 3-week futures contract for a railroad car of flax, which we would deliver in 3 weeks.

The gross dollars on that contract would be about $10,000-12,000, and it happened. I am sure that when Dad returned, he called the person I had dealt with to be sure the deal was as expected. He practiced due diligence.

By the way, we used standard railroad cars, so we'd have to put special wooden boards across each door, and wrap heavy, cheap brown paper around inside, since flax, unlike corn, was tiny and oily, and would flow out the cracks like water.

Of all the things I was responsible for, cleaning out barley from flat bottom bins was bad news since barley dust caused serious and lasting itchiness! Even today, when I open a box of Grape-Nuts, I smell that barley odor, and it brings to mind cleaning out barley bins. The milling operation caused a lot of dust, which accumulated in the driveway where farmers drove their wagon, trailer, or truck to have their ground feed discharged into their vehicle. Occasionally, an old guy with pigs to feed who lived on the other side of town came by and asked Dad if he could clean up the accumulated dust for his pigs, so he did. Later, he would give Dad a pint of dandelion wine. My dad did not like it, but took it. Later on, my cousin Jerry was visiting, and we saw a pint of wine on the shelf in our cellar, so we just had to taste it. It tasted like kerosene! Thank goodness we did not get sick or die!!

Rats

At about 12 years old, I had a .22-gauge bolt-action repeating rifle. On evenings when Dad was in the elevator office working on the accounts and books, I would be there to shoot rats. I got a penny a rat. This was okay, since I could get at least 48 to 50 rats with a box of shells I bought for 35 cents, a few cents profit. At least I had more money to buy shells, in comparison to those days I went hunting with cousins to wipe out gophers and was not paid at all. It was good fun, though.

Killing rats at the elevator was a continuing job. My shooting some was only a small part. With almost an infinite food supply, they proliferated wildly. Mainly, Dad had an exterminator come about twice a year. Since the elevator wasn't open on Sundays, he would usually gas them after work on Saturday nights. The idea was that no one should then be around for about 24 hours. The rats drew feral cats, so they probably got gassed too.

The Grain Markets

Over my years from about age 8 to 15, we occasionally went to visit relatives in Minneapolis. While there, my dad would take me along to visit the grain market; this is a regional market something like the Wall Street stock market, but for grains. A good deal of the market was for grain contracts for immediate and future delivery.

The people Dad dealt with to sell the grain he handled were market members who showed us around. Imagine a large room with benches or tables, with many pans of grain that were samples from railroad cars of grain to be sold individually at auction. The auctioneer was continually chanting as he sold each railroad car or cars of grain. Of course, the guy who represented my dad's offering was busy examining samples of grain and bidding on those he wanted for his customers. Dad's guy represented my dad's sales, and I am sure that people who needed grain—like mills buying wheat to make flour and companies that converted grain into other products like chemicals—were there buying grain.

Another aspect of the grain market was the futures market. This market had contracts to deliver grain in the future. These futures contracts could be designated for any time in the future. For example, a miller producing flour had wheat delivered on a schedule. This kept the mill running and producing flour to deliver to their customers, bakeries large and small, or for retail sales in grocery stores.

As with any group of businessmen, grain elevator managers had an association, and my dad participated in it. Usually they got together once a month. Typically, the meeting started at about 7:30 PM, allowing them to get off work, have supper, and then meet at a central location—maybe 20 to 50 miles away. When I was about 15 years old, I chose to go along with Dad since the meeting was only about 20 miles away in Appleton. There was a good movie playing there, so Dad would go to the meeting while I saw the movie. On the way, the car lost its fan belt and boiled most of the water out of the car radiator. Fortunately, we had a spare fan belt along, and the incident happened near a full slough—in Maryland, we call this a pond. So we got water from the slough in a bottle, filtered it through an old cloth rag, filled the radiator, put on the spare belt, and were on our way. We got there about 20 minutes late. I never attended those meetings, but afterward, my dad told the family about the details.

One thing I remember over the years was that Dad was always down on managers who got into speculating in the grain market. These managers often lost everything. Either they were gambling with their money (if they owned the grain elevator) or they illegally gambled with the money owned by the co-op members or company shareholders. Generally, if the business was worth $30,000 or $50,000, the gambling losses were multiples of that, so the poor sucker would lose his house, car, and savings, and be thousands of dollars in debt. Since my dad was a licensed grain buyer and weighmaster, he was bonded for $40,000—a vast sum in those days. Dad had come back to Bellingham in 1932 to get the elevator out of about $10,000 in debt. In retrospect, I understand why my dad was strongly against gambling. It was probably because he saw what went on in the business world after coming from the farm to that life at about age 21.

There is a story kinda related to that, possibly involving gambling or illicit activity. About 1940, my Uncle Frank and family were visiting from New York. Frank hung around the elevator with Dad at work so they could visit. The auditor was there going through the business records. My dad introduced Frank as an IRS agent, and my dad said the auditor went white. Afterward, Dad and Frank wondered what caused that reaction, but they never found out.

❧ *Chapter 9* ❧

World War II Starts

Things were getting better by October 1941, even to the point that my dad was considering buying a new car, but did not. Two months later, on December 7th, 1941, World War II began. No more new cars because of rationing, and we were later left running a dairy operation with a worn-out old car for all our needs, including hauling hay and moving cattle—a car with bald tires. What an innovative adventure we were on! Imagine—four bald tires, and using the car as the primary truck/tractor! During World War II, we often had only four tires, no spare. To keep going, we bought used tires that had replacement treads. It was also imperative to carry jacks, tire patching stuff, and boots—specially made pieces curved to fit inside the tire—to patch a hole in a tire. We never knew when a tire would fail and we would have to stop and repair it, day or night, good weather or a rain or snow storm. Even if that made us late for important events, what choice did we have?

Chapter 10

Mom the Farmer

While living in Bellingham, Mom was the farmer. Dad knew all about farming, but Mom and we kids were the doers. We had the chicken operation, hog operation, multiple gardens to sell stuff such as strawberries, and we eventually started the dairy operation. Imagine selling strawberries for a nickel a quart and, in one summer, taking in about $125. Mom was a good businesswoman, so the family accumulated money to go toward Dad's dream of a grocery business, where he would be the boss and butcher.

Mom told me that when she and Dad were first married, she expected that she was marrying a rich farmer's son, and she expected to be a farmer's wife. I think she was startled that, within a year, she was a grain elevator manager's wife living in town. I think it worked out, though, that from 1924 to 1945, the family lived on the edge of town—first in North Dakota and then in Bellingham—with a lot of land for gardens and barns for cows, pigs, and chickens, so she could be the "farmer," while Dad worked in the elevator.

Chapter 11

Before the Dairy

In 1939, when I was 12, we were visiting Aunt Mary Roggenbuck, Dad's aunt, for Sunday dinner. Mary's son, Dad's cousin, was discussing their farm. It came up that they had an elderly milk cow that they expected to send to the slaughterhouse in St. Paul, since it was not fit to be in their milk cow herd.

After some discussion, the men decided that since the cow was doing quite poorly, it would be brought to our place in Bellingham, and I would take care of it. We had two cows already, but I could stake it out along the railroad track where there was plenty of good grass. I would have to water it, carrying buckets of water from the well, and feed it ground feed waste cleaned up from the milling area where ground grain was loaded into wagons. For the milk of my cousin's cow—my pay—I had to take full care of our family's two milk cows. I kept my one cow's milk separate, separated the cream, and sold it to the creamery in town. The skim milk went to the family's pigs. That summer, besides taking care of three cows, I had a paper route for a Minneapolis paper, delivering to about 35 daily customers. (That was pretty good, since there were only 200 people in town, and a classmate of mine had about the same number of customers.) I saw this as the preamble to doing my part in the Bellingham milk business. Eventually my sister Gerry took over the paper route.

☙ Chapter 12 ☙

The Dairy Business

After World War II started, a widow who lived on the other side of Bellingham had her son drafted into the army. The widow and son had provided milk for the town, and everyone wondered, Who would provide the milk? Our family discussed it a lot and decided that my mom, Katie, Gerry, and I would do it. (Ralph was in the army, Don was in college, and Rusty was just a little kid.) So about 1942, we bought the business and the cows, and went at it.

Dad was not a farmer, but he had spent his life up until he married living on a mostly self-sufficient farm, so he knew all about farming. Over the next several months, Dad and I, with the help of the rest of the family, put stanchions—stalls—and manure gutters into the barn, installed an automatic watering system for the cows, set up a milk-handling system in the cellar in the house since we had an outside entrance, got hay, and put up fences—everything we needed to be a dairy farm.

By the time I was 17, I had a car, and I got $13 a month to handle the feed grain, alfalfa hay, and cornstalks, to clean the barn, and to feed and water the cows. My mom and I did the milking, my sisters and mom processed the milk, and my sisters delivered it and collected the money.

ELECTROCUTION

Soon after we got into the dairy and milk business, my dad got electrocuted because of an error in wiring for a 220-volt skid motor to run a conveyor that would put grain in a separate steel storage bin. Dad was up the ladder. I was holding the ladder and it happened. The electric bolt went into his left butt and out his foot, causing burns. (The arc didn't touch me at all since the ladder was made of wood.) I was 15 at the time so I took him to the doctor and on to the hospital in Madison, Minnesota, 10 miles away. After milking and doing the chores and supper I went back to see him and brought a carton of cigarettes. He said to throw them in the trash—he had decided to quit smoking. Four years later, I was helping check out after a stressful day in his grocery store in St. Cloud, and he was going through the routine of checking his pockets for a cigarette without thinking. I told him to go ahead and smoke a durn cigarette if his habit was so overpowering. He said no, and did not.

While Dad was laid up for about a month, we found a young war veteran who was kept out of the army because of an injury. He was getting started in the farming business and needed money, so he was eager to run the elevator. Since he knew nothing about it, I had to show him the ropes. I took off a few afternoons from school to help him out. Dad was only about a quarter of a block away, bedridden at home, so within minutes he could answer any question that came up.

BLIZZARD

While Dad was recovering from his electrocution, one Sunday morning my sister Katie and I went off with a family friend to Mass at Rosen. There was a blizzard, so we got stuck about a mile and a half along the way, went to a farmhouse of friends to get extra gloves and jackets, and walked the 2 miles home. That was not the end of it—the early blizzard was unexpected, so I had to get our dairy cattle fixed up to stay mainly inside barn quarters. This involved bringing the barn water system into operation for winter, housing the chickens, providing warmer straw for the pigs and hay for the cattle now in the barn—what a busy Sunday!

Ben Kelzer Helps with Cows

In the late 1930s and into the 1940s, my dad and mom were good friends with the Ben Kelzer family who lived on a dairy farm near Rosen. A major form of recreation for both couples was going to public and private dances, particularly wedding dances. (See Part 2 for more information on recreation for Dad and Mom.)

In later years in Bellingham, my folks would be at a dance and since I had a car, I would be there with a friend. Katie too was old enough, so she might be on a date with a high school friend, and she might have chosen to go to the same dance. I was very democratic; I would even dance with my mother sometimes. Of course, she would advise me on what I was doing wrong. I learned to dance mainly with high school girls who went to dances to learn to dance and to meet other girls and guys.

When Dad and Mom and the Kelzers got together, Ben would tell stories. In those days, he could have been on the radio. He could go on for 2 hours or more, never telling a story over, and never saying anything derogatory or demeaning, particularly about women, who were often the butt of jokes in those days.

After we got into the dairy business, we could always count on Ben to help and advise us on questions about our cows and other livestock. He helped with such things as castrating the male piglets, aiding a cow in the birth of a calf, and with the problems afterward.

It was a mutually beneficial arrangement for the two families. For example, on one occasion in the 1940s, there was a bad storm and many of the telegraph poles along the railroad were down. The railroad decided to discontinue using the telegraph, so Dad had me borrow a trailer and collect as many old telegraph poles as possible. (The railroad depot agent worked across the tracks, and he gave his okay.) We piled these poles in our barnyard and used them for building an outside corn stalk feeder for our cows—about ten of them by then. The best of the poles went to the Kelzer farm for a pole shelter by the barn. They were covered with a fresh-thrashed straw pile and became a winter shelter for part of his herd of milk cows. This was used as extra space to keep a number of extra cattle beyond his barn's capacity. This was common practice in our area by most dairy- and cattlemen.

Finally, another way we helped each other was that since we regularly had newborn calves, Ben Kelzer had first right to purchase the heifers—females—to get new blood lines into his dairy herd.

Jim Kelzer – Square Pegs in Round Holes

Here is a Kelzer story that may seem to have nothing to do with my dad John, but it did!! The oldest son in the Kelzer family, Jim—from little on—helped on the farm. He was about 2 years older than me. I was visiting the Kelzers on a Sunday once when he was about 16. He told me that all his riding on a plow or cultivator seat, looking at the rear end of the two mules, got quite old after about 2 hours. He figured there was more in the world and life than that. He did not want to be a square peg in a round hole. At about 18 or 19, he went to live in Watertown, South Dakota, to become an auto mechanic. He was the family mechanic, as I was in my family, and had an old car to practice on besides the family truck, car, and farm machinery. He was a good mechanic and a quick learner. In those days, it was common practice for a young lad to work as an "apprentice" to a garage owner to learn the business—for a small salary.

So later on, when I graduated from high school, I decided to be a chemist to leave shoveling manure behind.

In 1945, my parents were making plans to leave Bellingham. The goal was either to buy a dairy farm or for Dad to go into the grocery business. They had a choice between a dairy farm in the area north of St. Cloud or a grocery store in St. Cloud. I was a senior in high school and realized that if they did buy the farm, I would be a part of their plans.

But my idea was that I would go to St. John's University, like my older brother Don was doing—no more farming for me. My mother wasn't too happy about that, but my opinion was that Dad had detested farming earlier, and he would not be happy doing it now. So Dad and I voted for the store, and Mom's idea of farming was rejected. I am sure my dad recognized how his brother Wilbert had been chosen to be the farmer, and it was obvious he did not have an interest in that. While I was growing up, Wilbert the farmer spent a lot of time fixing cars and welding stuff. Grandma Ida was not too happy that he didn't concentrate on farming, but the saying is, "Don't try to put square pegs in round holes."

I often told my own kids "Find out what you like to do, do it, and you will get good at it. Find a job at it, and you can play at it for the rest of your life and get paid. Don't try to put square pegs in round holes."

Chapter 13

To St. Cloud

Moving to St. Cloud

With this family dairy business and my dad's job in the elevator 8 to 10 hours a day, six days a week, we accumulated some money, so my dad, mother, and sisters moved to St. Cloud. I had nearly finished high school so I stayed behind. In St. Cloud, Dad went into the grocery business. As long as I had known him, Dad had owned a farm near Parshall, North Dakota, which he kept as a financial asset. So he sold it to pay for part of the grocery business. I asked him why he got so little for the farm, since its land had coal outcroppings. He explained that he did not have the mineral rights.

We Sell the Dairy Business

When we left Bellingham to move to St. Cloud, we sold the milk business to Mr. Yonker, the town butcher who had a farm near town. We had an auction and sold a lot of the milk business equipment, and also stuff from the house we did not need anymore. Included in that was some children's play furniture my dad had built, such as tables, chairs, a kitchen sink, and a stove. I found out later that the children's furniture had been purchased by the farm family I stayed with near Bellingham, while I finished my last months of high school.

Ray Stays Behind

The farm family was a young couple who could not have kids. So one weekend while I was staying with them, I did the milking, feeding the pigs, and other farm tasks while they went off to Minneapolis, collected a newborn babe, and adopted her. They brought her home, and, after about 2 days of the baby crying, I finally told the mother to pick her up and hold and cuddle her as I showed her. I explained that I grew up with three sisters younger than me, and that the last one had been unhappy and obstreperous from the start, and that I had been old enough to help take care of her. I picked up the new babe and she quieted down, so I handed her to the new mother to do likewise, and she did.

Many years after that, in 1987, I met the couple at the Bellingham 100-year anniversary. I heard from them that they had bought a set of a little toy stove, sink, kitchen cabinet, table, and chairs that Dad had made for my sisters. They had been bought by the couple at our auction for their expected adopted daughter. While their daughter was growing up, the little girl played house with the toy stove, sink, cabinet, and chairs. She had gone off to college and then got a job in a bank in Minneapolis. She had taken her "toys" along with her to have for her own daughter when she married. The bad news was that while she was on vacation, the apartment house got sold, and everything in the basement storage—including the toys—was taken to the dump.

Chapter 14

St. Cloud – 1945 to 1989

Dad and the Grocery Store

After moving to St. Cloud, Dad quickly developed a routine as grocery store operator and butcher. The previous owners helped in the store for a brief period to train Dad in buying all the items sold there, dealing with the wholesale suppliers, and keeping records. Being a businessman prior to the store operation and already having changed jobs twice, Dad transitioned smoothly into his new role. As my sisters grew, they would replace store employees as needed. I was 18 at the time, and my sister Katie was 17. Ever since she was little, her goal in life was to be a storekeeper. So she was soon helping Dad with buying, maintaining the store's stock, and waiting on customers. She was Dad's right-hand "man."

Early after he arrived in St. Cloud, Dad helped my mother Marie's parents in a house that was more than they could handle. Dad made time for such things as getting up early on winter mornings to get their furnace running for the day, before going home for breakfast and opening the store at 8 AM. He also looked after things at Grandpa's such as changing the window screens to storm windows in the fall and back to screens in the spring, and fixing the car when it would not start. Of course, we children would be asked to help Grandpa and Grandma as the need arose.

Dad's hours in the store were often longer than in the elevator. Typically, the store was open 8 AM to 9 PM Monday through Saturday, and about 10 AM to 1 PM Sundays. He had employees, so he could take care of other things as needed.

Dad had a number of customers who called in orders because they couldn't go out—like little old ladies, or moms with kids where the husband was at work. He liked the delivery job and had a chance to see or even visit a while with customers. He used our old 1937 Ford for deliveries. (It was probably on its second or third 100,000 miles!) The car was using a lot of oil, so my dad made a deal with the gas station across the street. If they would save oil-change oil that still looked pretty good, he would pay them 5 cents a quart. He kept only adding oil—no oil changes for this old car.

In certain circumstances, Dad also used the car to get supplies for the store. For example, he would pick up a quarter beef or a half pork, avoiding wholesale delivery costs. Hackert Grocery was on the corner of 9th Avenue and 10th Street, in a suburban area with businesses on all four corners. Across the street was a grocery store, Dad's main competitor. Most customers could walk to the store, or husbands shopped on the way home from work—just like around Bellingham, where everybody knew everyone else.

HELPING DAD WITH THE STORE

In 1945, when my folks moved to St. Cloud, I was a freshman at St. John's University and lived on campus. I had a car so I could come home frequently, but normally I was very busy. During World War II, many high school teachers were drafted. So I had to catch up mainly in math once I got to college. Later in my college years at St. John's, I lived at home and could help Dad in the store to some extent.

Once, I went to pick up a quarter beef and asked at the wholesale meat place what that room was, with meat hanging in there that looked kinda green. I knew it wasn't a freezer, but I had never seen one of these. They said it was an aging room where they produced meat that they sold to restaurants. The green was part of the aging process that would result in very tender steaks.

42

At times when the grocery store was running low on eggs, Dad asked me to go to the wholesaler and get his order. Normally they would deliver, but I expect Dad paid for the delivery. I was asked to do this as needed with soft drinks, canned goods, and butter, among other items.

One of the interesting errands went like this: Dad saw an ad that a big chain store down on Main Street was selling butter by the pound for a little less than what Dad paid wholesale. Dad asked me to go buy 50 pounds of the butter. The sale was a come-on, as customers were limited to 3 pounds. So I bought 3 pounds, took the butter to the car, came back and bought 3 more pounds. I did this repeatedly. After a while, the store people objected; they knew what I was doing. So I loudly complained, "I am a customer! Here is my money!" And they sold it to me!! After that, I went through more times, and if they objected, I held up my money and the butter and carefully raised my voice. After all, they were undercutting the price of butter compared to most stores in St. Cloud. I hope other stores did as we did. It all worked out, and Dad got his allotment of butter at the lower price.

A story my dad liked to tell was about a 4-year-old from about four houses away. She would come to the store with a list from her mom and a few pennies for her to get candy. Typically, the little girl would pick out something for 6 cents, but would only have 4 cents. Dad would negotiate for a while, and then he would finally agree that the candy would be on sale next Saturday, so he would give her the sale price. I heard 20 years later that this little girl, now grown up, drove 50 miles out of the way to come to Hackert Grocery and introduce her two little girls to Mr. Hackert, my dad.

I have explained how I would get various supplies for the store. The reason I did was that wholesalers delivered once weekly, but often Dad ran short on things like bananas, eggs, canned soup, soft drinks, and butter. Besides, there was always a delivery cost to be avoided.

Much of the grocery business was done on credit, where customers would pay by the week or month, often because the breadwinner in the family was paid by the week or month. Just as in Bellingham while I was growing up, regardless of who bought the groceries, they were usually paid for at the end of the month.

This store credit business had a negative aspect too: bad debts. An example was a customer, a lawyer who apparently lived at about 130 percent of his income, but lived quite well, having a new car every other year, for example. He would consistently have a bill of about $300-500 at the store, paying just enough to allow him to keep buying. When my dad retired at 65, he was stuck with about $347 of the man's unpaid debt.

After retiring from the grocery store, Dad worked part time helping to run the parking lot for a major store in downtown St. Cloud. Dad had a lawyer friend who would occasionally stop by to shop, and Dad and he would go over to a nearby bar, taking off to have a beer and discuss local things.

When his lawyer friend heard of Dad getting stuck with the $300-plus debt, his response was, "He is a scoundrel, bilking a lot of people out of money." So the lawyer asked to take on the payment of the debt. Dad's friend started, and did a typical gung-ho collection job. Dad's friend used various ways to collect the bad debt and would get small amounts like $35 each time. His friend of course charged Dad nothing. But for about 3-1/2 years, every time the scoundrel paid something and the friend was shopping and parked in the lot, the two would celebrate by going for a couple of beers. It turned out to be a regular social event, a half-hour break in the middle of a busy day, maybe two or three times a month. And they would celebrate the justice of this bad guy having to finally pay off at least one of his debts.

LIVING AT HOME DURING MY COLLEGE YEARS

During my last 3 years at college, I lived at home. I would often come by the store at quitting time—9 PM—and would go out for a few drinks with my dad and discuss family things, politics, and business. In later years, I would try to do this father-and-son stuff with my sons.

During my last 2 years of high school and 4 years of college, I spent the summers working at the Del Monte canning factory in Sleepy Eye, Minnesota, about 100 miles south of St. Cloud. The objective was to accumulate enough money each summer to pay my college expenses, including college fees, room, and board. Since the pay at Del Monte was minimal, between packs I would go out harvesting in Minnesota and South Dakota. Several times while at Del Monte, they allowed workers to buy "dents," cans of corn or peas that were dented in handling and were sold for 5 cents per can. When I came to St. Cloud, I would bring them along for use by the family. They were not labeled, but because I'm a curious guy, I knew the codes on the cans given at the canning machines. For example, premium peas were about half-size, very tender and sweet, and their code was QZ. So that is what I mostly bought. From time to time during the sweet corn pack, when I would go home I would bring along two to three sacks of sweet corn right out of the field. Dad could sell that at the store.

Fixing Cars with Dad

Another story from my college days was when I was driving Don's Plymouth on a wintry Sunday morning and slid into another car on ice at the corner by Hackert Grocery. Don helped to get replacement parts from a car junkyard and, with Dad's advice, we removed the crumpled fender by using a chisel to break the welds. The "new" fender had holes along the sheet metal edge. Since we did not have welding equipment, we fastened it with stove bolts. In those days, my sister Katie was dating Vern—an auto repair guy. So we got Vern to paint it black—no problem matching that.

When I was about a junior in college, Don's car had noisy engine connecting rods. So I ordered all the parts—pistons and connecting rods, and rod bearings—from Sears. Guess what? They sent one and then another order, even though we only paid for one. We parked the car over a small ditch next to the garage, so we didn't have to jack up the car to get under it to do our work. With Dad's help and advice over about 2 weeks—he'd worked on his own cars since about 1921—we took things apart and installed the new parts in the engine. Since we had two sets of parts, we used the best fitting ones and then sent the extra set back to Sears. We had to buy a few tools, like a ring compressor to hold the rings to the piston, so the piston could be inserted into the cylinder hole in the engine block. After that the car ran fine, even making a long trip to New York and Washington, DC, to visit relatives in about 1948. The car ran well enough until Don bought a new car after he got a job and married Patricia. Then Ralph had the car for a number of years after that.

Helping Dad Around the House

I graduated from St. John's in 1949 along with my brother Ralph. He had been in the army from 1941 to 1945 and in an army engineering class during the war. He wanted to be a teacher, so he completed 4 years at St. John's. That summer, I worked my 6th year at Del Monte, and then went off to the University of Detroit for graduate school.

After a year there, I was home in St. Cloud for the summer and painted my dad's house. The house was a full two stories, with 8- or 10-foot ceilings upstairs and downstairs. The house was at the top of a hill, so the back of the basement floor was at ground level. To paint the back side, which was a full three stories high plus the peaked roof enclosing the attic, my dad built a scaffolding on that side of the house on which we placed the ladder. It went up two-and-a-half stories and reached nearly to the peak of the roof. That was the most difficult side of the house to paint, but the scaffolding worked.

Another project that summer was to move a single block of cement steps that had served as an entrance to a porch and to the kitchen. My brother Ralph had rebuilt the kitchen and closed off that kitchen entry. We wanted to be able to walk around the side of the house on a sidewalk level with the doorway which led to the top of the basement stairs. To make that possible, we needed to turn the steps around 180 degrees, move them toward the garage, and lower them about five steps.

Later, when I worked at DuPont, I discovered this was the kind of job for "riggers," who lift extremely heavy objects using cranes or derricks or chain hoists. Dad, Ralph, and I figured out how to do this, and did it with crowbars and ropes. When we were finished, one could walk across the sidewalk beside the house, and instead of going up the stairs into the kitchen, one could go down the stairs to the garage level, about the level of the basement floor. As I remember, Dad gave me a token payment of $50 for gas for the car and Saturday night dances at the east side fairgrounds. This was good training for me to use decades later, when Barbie and I had our own house to maintain and fix up while our kids were growing.

VISIT FROM THE FRANK HACKERT FAMILY

John and Marie would come visit to see the new babies and check on the grandkids as they were growing up. Of course, we regularly flew or drove out from the Eastern Shore to St. Cloud to see the old folks, relatives, and friends.

One interesting situation happened in the 1970s. Uncle Frank Hackert from Phoenix was visiting his kids and grandkids on Long Island, New York, and called me to find out where my dad John was. This was because he was going home by way of St. Cloud, but was surprised that my dad and mom were visiting us in Salisbury, Maryland. Frank, Frank's son Tom with his wife, Paula, and Frank's daughter Marilyn with her husband John flew down to Baltimore, rented a car, and drove to Salisbury. It was interesting to see Dad and Frank sitting on the couch in our living room, talking for hours about their early days, business, politics, and families.

Meanwhile, my cousins and I went to the beach and did other touristy stuff on the Eastern Shore. Tom was the airline pilot, and he knew Salisbury from the air, since pilot check flights sometimes brought him to the Salisbury area before returning to New York. One evening, we went to supper at Peaky's Restaurant, noted for its Maryland fried chicken. Dad and Frank kept their own conversation going, even when the rest of our crowd talked of other things.

The Traeger Farm

After moving to St. Cloud in 1945, Dad and Mom's social life continued at about the same pace as it did in Bellingham. One of the earliest things they did was to join the Newcomers Club, and later a seniors' group. Typically, they had activities like dinners and dances once or twice a month. About when my Number Three daughter, Janet, was a junior in college, she decided that she would work on a farm to see if that was a serious interest of hers. I told that to Dad, and at one of their dinner meetings, he brought the subject up. A couple across the table had a daughter whose family was interested in having a person work on their dairy farm near Albany, Minnesota, for the next summer. To Janet, this was the best possibility since many times I had told her stories of my dairy work growing up. The alternative was possibly working on Ray's cousin's farm near Rosen and Bellingham.

This was the beginning of the Ray Hackerts and Jim and Sandy Traeger family's friendship. I remember Janet getting on the phone with Sandy during their first contact. They talked a long time—Ray was paying the phone bill—and they decided to get together for a profitable summer for both.

Later, Janet was in graduate school at the University of Minnesota, only about an hour's drive to the farm. Janet eventually became godmother for a new baby boy born to the Traegers. At that time, she was getting a Master of Science in agricultural engineering. From what

I heard, the Traeger's grandma was a Rademacher—probably a shirttail relative to my uncle and cousins on the farm near Bellingham.

Later, when my Number Four daughter, Carol, worked at "the farm" and when she was at St. Ben's and St. John's, she considered the Traeger home as her "other home." This was useful since, at that time, Barbie was recovering from brain surgery, so our two younger daughters weren't getting much guidance from Barbie. I even told Sandy Traeger that she was my younger daughters' other mother, so she should "kinda" help them on the right road of life. In those days and for years, the families visited back and forth, and were together for weddings and funerals—a real extended family.

John Retires – about 1970 until 1989

Between 1940 and 1945, my mom often complained that Dad should quit the grain business because he had a bad cough. It did not improve over several years after he got electrocuted, even though he had stopped smoking. This electrocution was his second serious work injury. During the Depression years with hardly any crops, in about 1933, the government sent hay into Bellingham to feed farmers' horses and cows. Dad was opening railroad cars and a loose bale in the doorway hit him in the head, jarring his neck. He had a sore neck the rest of his life.

Later in life, when he retired, my dad sold his grocery business to my sister Katie. This was appropriate since Katie, from high school on, helped in the store. Even when she was little, she always played "grocery store."

Shortly after retiring from the grocery store, my dad and mom went to visit the Don and Patricia Hackert family in Palisade, Nebraska, for a month. Apparently, the kids thought it was a good idea to have them around that long. Patricia said Dad even spaded her garden to get it ready for planting flowers and vegetables. The grandkids were still mostly at home, so they could go on various adventures and enjoy activities like playing cards and going to nearby beaches for swimming.

Back in St. Cloud, Dad kept very busy. Various activities my dad was good at, mostly later in retirement, included helping my mother with dolls for orphaned children, making quilts for the missions and for their children and families, and helping the hungry by cooking in their parish program.

For the orphan children, Mom and Dad would collect abandoned dolls with the aid of many other people. My dad would recondition each doll by repairing arms or affixing heads. My mom would buy unwanted wigs, and then my dad would separate them and attach them to the dolls' heads. The "hair" was chosen so the little girl getting the doll could fix its hair, comb it, and style it. By the middle of December, in time for Christmas, the boxes of dolls would be given to the local orphanage.

Quilting went on year-round, with one of the church's women's groups making quilts for missions. There were specialties like choosing the design, cutting and sewing the pieces together to make the pattern, and finally quilting it. This involved Mom or a group of women sewing the padding part of the quilt between the front upper pattern and the plain backing. My dad knew how to set up a quilting frame for Mom or other ladies to do the quilting. Mom's specialty was sewing the quilt pattern pieces together. Both Mom and Dad did all the steps in making quilts for family members.

A story about that: I was a sophomore in college and arrived home about 4:30 one afternoon. My mother and grandma were there, and they wanted me to buy a chance on this quilt for the missions. I had about two quarters in my pocket, and finally I yielded and took a chance—25 cents. They sold chances since they got more money that way than just selling the quilt outright. About a month later, low and behold, I won the quilt. What did a 20-year-old need with a quilt? I lived at home and Mom provided all the bedding I needed. (I never thought to donate it back to them so they could raffle it off again.) My mom said she would save it for me in case I married and could use it; and she did.

Another story: I was home at St. Cloud, visiting with Barbie and our family, and Mom and Dad showed me a quilt they had recently finished for my son Eric, for when he got married. Later Eric came by, and he had already gotten into his car to leave when my mom asked him to wait. She got the quilt out and gave it to him, explaining that winter was coming on and it got down to 15 to 25 degrees below zero in Madison, Wisconsin, where he was going to graduate school, so he could start using the quilt now.

My wife, Barbie and I got a quilt from my folks that was made from pieces of cloth left over from dresses my mom made for my sisters over the years when they were growing up. Barbie would put that quilt on our bed to show visitors, and I would point out, for example, that the cloth in a certain quilt patch was left over from a dress made for my sister Katie when she was a freshman in high school.

In retirement, my dad and mom helped to prepare dinners for the poor in St. Cloud at their church. Once, I arrived home on a Friday afternoon and they were not home, so I went to visit them at the church center. They were in charge of making a batch of 40 to 50 gallons of mashed potatoes. My mom was feeling quite poorly, so she would have Dad bring her a spoonful from the big mixer to taste. Then she would say, "John, go put in another pound and a half of butter so we can see if that brings the taste up to good or perfect."

After my dad retired and lived on the north end of town, one time a duck nested in my mother's flowers along the side of the house. Mom and Dad called the local paper and had a photographer come take pictures. Once the eggs hatched, the photographer came back and took more pictures as the mother duck walked the babies down the road, with the police helping to stop traffic.

DAD'S (AND MOM'S) RETIREMENT HOME

Late in life, my dad and I talked about giving up the house and garden and getting an apartment, since both he and Mom were getting to the point where they could not handle the house chores like shoveling snow, cutting grass, and caring for the garden. Dad had looked at the Benedict Center, which had apartments with a garden plot that Mom and Dad could care for, a meal plan so that apartment cooking could be minimal, and a nursing home associated with the apartments, if that was eventually needed. Also, there were retired priests there, so there was daily Mass. It sounded to him like a good place for them to live.

My wife Barbie and I came to visit one time, and my mother wanted me to go with her to look at the Benedict Center. Thinking of what Dad and I had discussed, and knowing Mom could be contrary, I pretended to dislike the idea and told her, "Why do you want to leave the house, where you have room for us to come visit, a garden, a garage for the car, a sewing room, and everything you need?" A little later that day, as expected, my brother Ralph came home, and Mom asked him to take her to Benedict Center, and he did. When they came back, Mom was all excited to move there. Finally, Dad agreed "reluctantly." (He had been pushing the move with me, but was sure that if it was not Mom's own idea, she would not agree.) So it was done.

John Dies – March 1989

From as early as I can remember, before I was even 5 years old, I recall my dad having outbreaks of yellow jaundice. He would develop a somewhat yellowish complexion and would feel poorly for a few days, and then was all right again.

By the time he was in his late eighties, he was diagnosed with a bile duct restriction. This was not particularly very serious then, since the doctor could do outpatient operations in his office and could relieve his symptoms. He explained, though, that he could not correct the problem, since to operate, he would have to move several major organs out of the way to get to the bile duct. This was an acceptable operation if he were still 30 or 50 years old, but at his age, "the cure is worse than the disease."

When doctors did that operation on an older person, most of the time the patient died. Based on Dad's age, the doctor also predicted that he could restore the bile duct only three times. He predicted Dad's death in about 3 years.

He was correct to within 3 weeks. The doctor told us that when the bile duct became blocked, the visible symptom was yellow jaundice. If blocked completely, a human can live 3 days plus or minus. The bile duct feeds bile into the intestines, where it functions to aid in completing food digestion (as a surfactant and chelating agent). If no bile enters the intestinal tract, the intestines degrade from the inside, and one dies in about 3 days. I had heard that while studying biochemistry in college. I studied that since I occasionally needed special chelating agents in my work as a chemist.

In my thesis work in graduate school, I worked for a time with a chelating agent called ethylenediaminetetraacetic acid (EDTA). At that time, another student with whom I shared office space was working on porphyrins, chemicals that excess lead in the body combines with to solubilize lead and excrete it in one's urine.

It never occurred to me then, but I found out years later that EDTA was being fed to people that had lead poisoning, providing a quick cure. (I went to graduate school at the University of Detroit. Detroit had a number of lead battery factories and a high incidence of lead poisoning within its population.) My point in this story: Has anybody tried curing a bile duct blockage by feeding the patient ethylenediaminetetraacetic acid (or other chelating agents) to prolong life? Maybe Dr. Richard Kolodrubetz (my nephew) has the answer. This chelating agent is used freely: I have seen it listed as an ingredient in packaged food.

My dad John died in March 1989 at the age of 90-1/2. The funeral was during a snowstorm. As I remember, my daughter called the night before the funeral from Pittsburgh and said she was stuck there because of the snow. I suggested that she go to the Northwest counter and get a flight to Minneapolis. I explained that pilots made every effort to get home to Minneapolis (the hub for Northwest) and she finally arrived several hours later. They flew around northern Minnesota for a while until a runway was cleared and they could land in the storm.

Mom Dies after Dad

On December 12 of her last year, 1989, I was visiting Mom. She was very adamant that I take her out to Christmas shop for her grandchildren. I almost froze coming in from the car. I told her she must be crazy – "You're going to freeze to death if you go out in this!" It was 22 degrees below zero, and the wind was about 35 miles per hour. She died on December 25.

A Note About This Story

Of course, I have my own points of view like most people. For example, in the mid-years in St. Cloud, my nephew Richard Kolodrubetz taped video and sound of discussions with my dad John and mom Marie. Several years later, Barbie and I were visiting Patricia in Palisade, Nebraska. On the second or third evening, I suggested we watch and listen to the first of the reels. We probably spent 2 hours and only got halfway through it, because my dad's viewpoint about a lot of stuff he said about Bellingham led me to correct this story to convey the "real" situation.

PART 2

The Stories

About

My Dad John

Chapter 15

North Dakota Memories

After running the Farmers Elevator in Bellingham, my dad got a better job managing the grain elevator in Anamoose, McHenry County, North Dakota for about 8 years. The family moved to North Dakota in 1924.

My dad did all kinds of things to make money for the elevator. He sold at least three, but maybe five kinds of coal. The most sought-after was lignite from North Dakota. It was the cheapest coal available, so it was used the most. Everyone was poor, since North Dakota was having a drought. As I remember, Dad also sold specialty feeds for cattle, pigs, and chickens, and twine for harvesting to increase the company's income.

Our house in Anamoose, North Dakota was on the edge of town and at the end of a side street. The property of about an acre included the house, a barn for our cow, a place for chickens (plus a fence for them), a sidewalk between the house and barn, and space for pigs which we did not use. The house had a cellar with an outside entrance. On the side of the house away from town was a hill—a small rise—with a rock pile at the top, and beyond that, farmland.

The front of the house had a screened-in porch where Dad often took pictures of the kids, particularly the little ones, on Sunday afternoons. We usually entered the house by the back door which faced the barn. When going in, we went into an entryway which led to a set of unused attic stairs. Then we came to a generous kitchen, then went into the middle living room of the house that led to two bedrooms—one on the right and one on the left—and then walked through a sliding door to a room at the front of the house.

We would go to Midnight Mass on Christmas Eves, after being awakened following the children's 7 or 8 PM bedtime. On returning from Mass, we would go into the house, and the sliding door would be open. The Christmas tree would be lit, and everyone's presents were under the tree, not wrapped. The family tradition was to have candy, nuts, and food, and for the children to play with the new toys for a few hours, and then go to bed.

———◦◦◦◦◦◦———

During the decade from 1970 to 1980, all the kids born in North Dakota except for Don got together to visit Anamoose and friends such as the Rudnicks and Nitzes. Among others we visited were the Thoroughs, who had lived several houses away on our street. The son, Ralph's classmate in Anamoose, ran an auto repair shop and did a "Thorough" job at it.

The hill by the abandoned old house was now only a slight rise. The rock pile was still there, and a tree still stood in the middle of it.

———◦◦◦◦◦◦———

A personal memory: When I was a little kid, my dad would put me to bed and stay with me for a little while. I thought that was a good idea. I could hear our cow bellering, waiting to be milked, as I dropped off to sleep.

———◦◦◦◦◦◦———

I injured my eye and spent time at a hospital in Harvey, the next town. Every evening, Dad came by after work and brought a Hershey chocolate bar. I always saved part, and they lasted for weeks.

Later, at home from the hospital, Dad told me the doctor said that I probably would become blind in that eye. When he would change the bandage on that eye, I would purposely look carefully out the bedroom window to remember what I saw then.

Children at Play

From my earliest years in Anamoose, we played many games and with many toys. We had a small two-seater pedal-powered car for 2- to 5-year-olds that we pedaled back and forth on our short sidewalk. We also played croquet with wooden mallets and balls. At times, this was kinda deadly, but we all managed to survive.

The family had a garden, so all could help there. We often went up the hill to the rock pile to play there, of course. All us kids had toy trucks, cars, dolls, doll buggies, and more, to play with outdoors, or in the house in winter. I had a truck with electric lights, so I played with it in the dark.

Root beer

It was my dad's custom to make root beer for the family. We collected empty beer bottles, ketchup bottles, and other similar bottles for this. He would make a batch of root beer usually on a Sunday afternoon, and it would be stored in the cellar for several weeks to ripen. (During Prohibition—from 1920 to 1933—the Hackerts also made beer.) Late one night, I was awakened by what sounded like gunshots. Upon investigation, we found that the ripening bottles of root beer were exploding in the cellar. According to Dad, he had put too much "root beer makings" in the recipe!

—◦◦◇◦◦—

Our town was on a railroad main line so mostly the train did not stop. What was interesting was that the mail was picked up (and I suppose dropped off) at a post along the railroad with a hook catcher. As kids, we liked to see the train zip by and the mail catcher operate as the train passed.

—◦◦◇◦◦—

Once I was with my dad in the car going to the store. A horse that looked pretty poorly was plodding down the main street with its head hanging down. There was an old man on the horse who looked in poorer shape than the horse. Dad told me he was an Indian—the first one I'd ever seen.

—◦◦◇◦◦—

Mom and Dad had an adventure early in their life in Anamoose. Mom, along with her little ones, went to visit her stepdad, mom, brothers, and sisters on a horse ranch one state to the west, in Montana.

The train in our town went near the ranch, so it was easy to go there by train, and get off at Glendive near the ranch. Our family has a photo of Mom dressed up in chaps, a cowboy hat, and two holstered six-guns provided by her brothers. Grandpa Voigt was one of the Old West cowboys, but his short go at ranching failed, since the gasoline revolution had begun and, by about 1930, horses were almost worthless, being replaced by tractors, cars, and trucks.

—◦◦◇◦◦—

My folks had several relatives in North Dakota and many friends from the elevator business, church, and their community. One family with kids about my age was the Paul Rudnick family. We often visited back and forth and got to know them quite well. My friend at that farm was Lawrence Rudnick, who was about 2 years older than I was. When he was in first grade, he came home from school and he found no one at home. So he decided to go over to his uncle's place about half a mile down the road. It was very cold—maybe 10 to 15 degrees below zero—and snowing. By the time he got to his uncle's home, several fingers, his cheeks, and his nose were frozen. Eventually everything was fixed up and Lawrence healed, but it was a traumatic thing.

———◦◇◇◇◦———

In Anamoose, we went to church almost a mile away and outside of town. To get money to run our church, parishioners paid "pew rent." The Hackert family pew was about halfway up on the right side. I remember when my little sister Katie was about 1-1/2 or 2 years old, she got away from Dad and walked almost all the way up to the altar during Mass. My dad got up, walked slowly after her, and fetched her back to our pew. She was a wild kid.

———◦◦◇◦◦———

As a little kid in North Dakota, where we experienced so little rain, I would stand outside with my brothers and sisters whenever it clouded up to see if we could feel a few raindrops that might fall on our heads.

———◦◦◇◦◦———

Dad got the daily paper from Minneapolis-St. Paul, and one day they started a contest, so my dad joined in. Every day the paper had a block of numbers, maybe 25x25, and the puzzle was to connect the numbers, one to another, so there was a single continuous line of them, both up and down and left and right, and the goal was for them to add up to the maximum sum. This went on for a while—maybe 2 weeks or a month. Guess what? Dad won the contest! In those days, you could buy a nice car for $250. With the prize money, Dad bought a green 1928 Pontiac four-door sedan.

———◦◦◇◦◦———

Many times on weekends, Dad and our family would visit family and friends. We would also go for a drive in the car on many spring and summer evenings. I particularly remember the sights and smells of spring flowers, freshly mown hay, and flowering hay like alfalfa. We would drive by low spots where water would have stood earlier, but because of lack of rain, they had become dry alkali sloughs. These drives were very interesting in spring, when the little snow from winter brought out "zillions" of native prairie flowers (and weeds).

A family we visited when we still lived in North Dakota was the Steve Schreder family. Steve ran an elevator near where we lived, and he was my mother, Marie's, cousin. Steve and his wife had no children. Steve played the guitar and enjoyed playing for company so, in visiting back and forth, we got to hear a lot of good music like one hears in Western movies.

———◦◦◇◦◦———

One year, Dad worked out a partnership to raise flax on a planned fallow field next to our house. That land was owned by an elevator customer he knew. At some time in the spring, Dad saw him and remarked that it looked like he was not planning to plant that year. The farmer expected he would leave it fallow. Dad suggested that it would make a good field for flax. Dad would furnish the seed, the farmer would prepare the field, plant, take care of it, and harvest it—and they would each get half of the proceeds from the sale.

They got a very good crop of flax and got about $300 each, which was equivalent to several months of my dad's salary. He bought an Easy Electric Washing Machine, which had a big washer tank and a smaller spin-dryer tank. This was to aid in cleaning my dad's clothes from the elevator that got filthy dirty with all that grain dust. Mom had to do laundry for my dad, herself, and four children, so she probably appreciated the new washer/dryer. My dad probably had the idea from his dad who had bought Grandma Ida an electric washing machine for the washhouse years before.

———◦◦◇◦◦———

We lived in a house at the edge of town. On his way to the elevator, Dad walked a path across a wheat field next to our home. We kids were short enough so we could not see over the full-grown wheat. When we saw Dad coming from work, we would run out in the path to meet him.

———◦◦◇◦◦———

Once, when arriving back from a trip to the store, Dad tested the brakes as we drove up to the car shed. I was standing in front of the passenger front seat and I busted the windshield at the abrupt stop. In those days, the windshield was just plain glass, so I didn't cut my head, thank God. But of course, he was very apologetic! That didn't stop me from wanting to be on the go with him. Even in those days, I wasn't a sedentary person—I was a traveling person.

———◦◦◇◦◦———

One year, the big hotel in Anamoose had a fire; Dad helped fight the fire as a volunteer fireman. It was 10 degrees below zero and windy. After hours of firefighting, he finally came home. He was frozen in his coveralls and couldn't sit down. He had to stand for at least an hour, making a puddle of meltwater on Mother's kitchen floor.

———◦◦◇◦◦———

On each of his kids' birthdays, Dad brought home a box of Cracker Jacks for that kid. The adventure was the prize in the box! And then they'd get to eat the popcorn, too!

———◦◦◇◦◦———

BAD DOG

One summer afternoon, our 4-month-old puppy went after my mother's chickens that had gotten loose from the chicken pen, and killed one after another. With all the noise my mother came out, took a broom, chased and caught the dog, and tied it up by the barn. When Dad came home, he was directed by Mom to take care of the dog. Dad got a gunny sack, put two dead chickens in it, put the dog in it so his nose was in amongst the dead chickens, then whipped him with a folded newspaper until he was yelping and howling. Dad finally let him go. Thereafter, the dog ran whenever a chicken came close to him. My dad explained that he first thought to get the shotgun and blow the dog to smithereens, but then he realized the dog just did what came naturally to him. With Dad's gunny sack lesson, the dog learned something he never forgot, and could continue to be our family dog.

———◇◇◇◇◇◇———

Another remembrance from my earliest days in Anamoose: It was Grandma Ida's tradition to send us a fully processed goose for Christmas, ready to go in the oven. It came by mail a few days before Christmas.

———◇◇◇◇◇◇———

In 1932, we moved to Bellingham, Minnesota, for Dad to take a job again in the Farmers Elevator in Bellingham. Because of bad times, the Anamoose Board of Directors was going to cut his wages so he changed jobs. In moving, he talked to his cousin Steve Schreder and alerted him that he was leaving Anamoose, and that Steve might apply there when a vacancy was announced.

———◇◇◇◇◇◇———

My dad's good friends in Anamoose were the Rudnicks and the Bill Nitz family. For years after we moved to Minnesota, the Nitzes, who were wheat farmers, alternated living in North Dakota during the wheat planting and harvesting and in Florida during the winter. Many times in later years, they would stop off to and from Florida for a visit with my dad and mom in Minnesota. In later years, it was the custom for the John Hackert sons to stop by to see Bill Nitz whenever they were in

North Dakota. He commented once to my dad that we Hackerts came by more often than relatives like nephews.

———◦∞◇∞◦———

Several times while we lived in North Dakota, usually in the fall, my dad would take the family along and go visit his farm near Parshall, North Dakota. This is the farm given to Dad by Grandpa Peter when he married my mother Marie. The main thing, as I remember, was that Dad wanted to see how the guy running the farm was doing. Obviously, in drought years, there was little or nothing for him to sell to pay the rent. In those days, I suppose Dad was stuck with paying the taxes out of his own pocket.

One thing I remember vividly was that there were lignite coal outcroppings on the farm. I saw how the renter went to these outcroppings with a team of horses and wagon, pickaxe and shovel, and hauled coal to the house. He piled it up near the doorway so he had coal to heat the house all winter. (In North Dakota, the winters are often 30 to 35 degrees below zero, and the wind blows much of the time at 40 miles an hour. That's cold!)

———◦∞◇∞◦———

My mom asked Dad to buy her a new pair of sewing scissors, since the old pair was worn out. Dad went to the local store in Anamoose and asked for a left-handed pair of scissors, since Mom was left-handed. The store owner, who had been in the business for at least 2 decades, thought he was jesting. He didn't have any left-handed scissors and had never heard of such a thing. Dad suggested he get out his scissors catalog, and the store owner learned there was such a thing as that. Two weeks later, Mom had her scissors.

Chapter 16

John and Hunting – Father and Son Bonding

From when I was very little, even in North Dakota, where we lived until I was about 5 years old, I knew my dad had a Winchester 1898 12-gauge shotgun and that he'd use it when it was necessary. For example, our young dog who chased and killed my mother's chickens most likely would have been executed by Dad when he found out. He would have shot the dog with his shotgun. Thankfully, Dad found a better solution to teach the dog never to kill chickens again.

PHEASANT HUNTS

After we moved to Bellingham, Minnesota, my dad was again in the area where he grew up. Dad was a pheasant hunter from early youth. We never had a hunting dog, so as a young boy, I served that purpose. I chased up the hiding pheasants, he shot them, and I fetched them. It was not unusual on Sundays coming home from church that, if we saw a pheasant, we would stop with the whole family in the car, and Dad and I would get out to get it. There were usually enough pheasants about so that if we saw one, there were often others hiding in the grass, weeds, or cornfield.

Pheasant season was usually several weeks in late October. Hunting started at sunrise. Usually a legal limit in Minnesota was three birds. The preference was cocks, but the smaller hens were also taken. Obviously, the hens were needed to breed more pheasants, but as with chickens, one rooster went a long way among the hens.

I grew up as a hunter. By about age 10, I accumulated enough money to buy a .22-caliber bolt-action repeating rifle and used it often to hunt around the edge of our small town. I got familiar with almost all the land nearby—the empty hay barns, fields, creeks, ditches, fence rows, and groves of trees. I also got to know the people on these properties, like classmates' families, relatives, and people doing business with my dad in the elevator. And in later teenage years, I got acquainted with people we bought hay and corn stalks and occasionally milk and cows from, and with people who hired me to work on their farms. I was not the only young lad in our town who hunted as a pastime, but I seldom hunted with other lads since they were generally not safe with their guns. I learned early to never, never, ever point a gun at another person—even if the bolt was removed from the gun, or the gun was supposedly not loaded: That was when accidents happened.

Following are a few hunting stories to demonstrate my point on safety.

On a typical Sunday afternoon in the fall, our family would be visiting Aunt Mary Spors along with various uncles and aunts and, as they say, cousins by the dozens. After Sunday dinner, someone would suggest we go pheasant hunting, so we did. The system was that the adult men would line up about 10 to 20 yards apart. Usually, my dad John would be placed at the end of the line since he was a good shot. He had a 12-gauge gun with a full choke, so the shot held a tight pattern and far shots could knock down the bird. My young cousins and I were in between the shooters to scare up hiding pheasants. If the hunting tactics were organized right, a bird would abruptly take wing and go with the wind, and each man who was nearby got a shot at the flying bird. Dad was the cleanup shooter at the end of the line. During most such afternoons in 2 or 3 hours of hunting, almost every hunter got one or more pheasants. Often, by chance or ability, some guy got more than others did, but the take was usually divided evenly. Of course, a factor was that the legal limit defined the number of birds one could carry home regardless of how many they caught. In season, game wardens randomly and occasionally set up roadblocks and counted how many legal birds one had. In some cases, when people had too many birds in the car and not enough hunting licenses, birds were tossed out in the ditch while the hunters were waiting in the line before their vehicle got to the game warden inspection site. I suppose that some people who chose the easy way bought a hunting license and, instead of going to the trouble of hunting, worked the checkpoints to pick up discarded birds they could claim legally as theirs.

Another hunting story—about eight relatives from my mother's side came to Bellingham on an October Saturday for the first 2 days of pheasant season. We started out in the plowed field south of our house where about 400 pheasants were scratching and eating at sunrise. My dad had taken the day off from work; a fellow looked after the job for him so Dad could hunt.

In about an hour and a half, we had gotten enough birds to reach the limit for each hunter. Back to the house we went for a breakfast that my mom had probably spent an hour preparing.

By about 10 AM, everyone was fed so we went out again, but this time with cars, driving from field to field to find more flocks to pursue. By about 12:30 we came home again, everyone mostly reaching their limit of birds, and sat down to a "Mother Marie Big Dinner." We went out again at about 3 PM to repeat our hunting process. It was a success!

You'll notice that one hunter might get 3 times the limit in one day this way. But when it was time to go home, they did not want to be carrying more than their legal car limit, so we would be left with a lot of their extra birds!

In the afternoon, though, all realized that my somewhat older twin cousins had very different outcomes. Tom got a number of pheasants, but Roy, the hunter in that family, had none. So near the end of the day, if a bird flew up and Roy and someone else shot, we all agreed it was Roy's bird.

As far as I was concerned, I was old enough to use a shotgun, but it was customary to start with a 20-gauge gun. I had borrowed one from a friend of mine. A 20-gauge gun is not much better for its shot pattern than a .22-caliber rifle. I may have gotten one bird—by chance. This gun was all right for a bird sitting on the ground, but not very good for a rapidly flying bird.

I have a memory about hunting with Cousin Roy, who was on leave from the Air Corps around 1943 or 1944 so he came to the family hunt. He was a tail gunner on a B17 bomber that eventually was part of 1000 plane raids over Germany. During our hunt, Cousin Roy was not hitting his bird. At the time, I thought if all the tail gunners were like Roy, that World War II would be a long, long war. Of course, on the job, Roy was firing machine guns, and I think they had tracer bullets so one could see their trails and correct to hit an enemy plane.

By the way, and to contrast with Cousin Roy, after the war, I was in trigonometry class with his twin brother Tom, who had been a navigator on a B17 plane. He had a lot of problems with trig; I assume it was used to calculate proper navigation for planes, so I was surprised that his outfit came out of the war in one piece. Obviously, though, if you have a thousand-plane raid, you have a thousand navigators, so hopefully someone got navigation right. The problem was if one plane got shot up or had a bad engine, it had to get back to England alone, and that navigator had to know his business or die, along with the others in the plane.

So on Saturday, the hunting group had finished their hunt. Next day, we all went to Sunday Mass in Rosen, and to dinner, and then our guests left for home. As they departed, we were left with 38 birds. So the rest of the day was spent cleaning the birds, preparing the meat, and canning most of it to keep and eat later.

This type of family visit and pheasant hunting was also commonplace earlier in my dad's life. He told stories of how the Hackert relatives from Minneapolis/St. Paul and the Voigts would come to the Peter Hackert farm in the early 1900s. Dad's first cousins like Clint Hackert, who was Grandpa Peter's nephew, and Clint's brothers (policemen from St. Paul, Minnesota) would come on their motorcycles and have a hunt similar to those we had in Bellingham.

Another item that may be of interest is that the limit on the number of pheasants for hunting in the fall could vary some years. One can get an idea of what the pheasant population will be by the weather during the spring hatch of chicks. Like turkeys, young pheasant chicks are very vulnerable to rainy and cold springs until they lose their birth fuzz and form feathers. Then they can withstand cold weather and cold rain. Imagine that each pheasant hen has 7 to 13 chicks. If nearly all survive to full growth, one year's hatching provides plenty of birds for the fall pheasant hunt.

St. Paul – Milwaukee Relatives

I learned from Dad that when I was young, the relatives often came from Minneapolis/St. Paul in late October to visit Grandpa Peter and Grandma Ida on their farm near Bellingham to go pheasant hunting. When the Hackert clan arrived in Minnesota from Germany—now Central Poland—one faction settled near Bellingham, and another part of the family settled in St. Paul. Later, a portion of the St. Paul Hackert clan split off and moved to Milwaukee, Wisconsin. I heard this growing up since we would visit the St. Paul Hackerts when we were there on vacation over the years.

Around that time, as I remember, my dad's cousin Clint became chief of police in St. Paul. According to my dad, he told the gangsters who were known by Clint that they could leave St. Paul—or he, as police chief, would be sure that they'd be sorry for staying. They would be jailed even for minor offenses like spitting on the sidewalk, until the police had enough evidence to put them away for a long time. So St. Paul went through a quiet, safe period under Clint's leadership as chief of police.

In 1951, I moved to Delaware to work for DuPont and after a year or two, I met Charlie Hackert at our factory. We would have lunch together over the years, and from stories he told about his Hackert family coming to the USA, moving to St. Paul and then to Milwaukee, his history fit very well with my family's similar stories. Obviously, he was a long-lost cousin of sorts. Charlie lived in Federalsburg, Maryland, near our workplace.

Jackrabbit Hunts

A winter activity when I was growing up was to have a jackrabbit hunt about two to four times during the season. The first one was usually in about November, when the jackrabbits' fur had turned white to blend with the snow.

The hunt would be advertised mostly by word of mouth. On a given Sunday afternoon, usually at least four farm trucks would arrive on Main Street in Bellingham. The hunters divided up into four groups and got into the trucks.

They carefully chose a square mile section of land beforehand and surrounded it, with one of the groups on each side. The men and young people were spread out on each outer edge of the square mile. (Most "sections" in the Midwest were bounded by roads, so that was a handy place for the hunters to start.) At a signal (for example, two rapid gunshots by the leaders of the hunt), all hunters moved inward toward the center. The rule was to only shoot outward at jackrabbits (and foxes) that ran between hunters so that no one was shooting at another hunter. There was hardly any shooting at first, but as the hunt progressed, and if they were lucky, there would be much shooting toward the end, when the hunters ended up as an organized crowd in the middle.

All dead jackrabbits (and foxes) were carried back to the trucks to be counted and delivered to the shop in town that bought them. Of course, foxes were turned in to the county, since they were killed for the cash bounty on them—they were considered a pest. Maybe a few pheasants were taken illegally for personal use. The hunt rules were against that, and we did not need game warden supervision.

Jackrabbits were a problem for farmers. Think: "They bred like rabbits." Without many enemies, they would grow to about 30 to 40 pounds each, and, sitting at rest, the top of their ears came up higher than an adult guy's belly button. At the end of the jackrabbit hunt season, the money accumulated was used to hire a hall, a band, and kegs of beer. All were invited to the party and dance, and those recorded as members of the hunts did not have to pay admission. The other "guests" had to pay a fee to attend.

Bellingham and Lac qui Parle County were dry locations—no hard liquor allowed. When I attended one of the jackrabbit hunt parties during high school, I realized that one of the bootleggers of the hard liquor was one of our relatives!

Another hunt story involved when I visited my uncle Wilbert on the Peter Hackert farm when I was in college. Wilbert was plowing, so I drove out to the field and waited until he stopped at the end of a row. We talked a short while, then he got on the tractor seat and started across the field. After about 50 yards, a pheasant popped up and started running across the plowed field. Wilbert stopped, grabbed his .22 rifle, and shot three times. The first shot hit about 5 or 6 inches behind the pheasant, the second shot raised dirt around its feet, and the third shot was heard coincident with the bird rolling in the dirt, dead. Of course, Wilbert had an automatic, so the sounds were a rapid bang–bang–bang. Wilbert brought me the pheasant to give to Aunt Margaret for their supper.

It was customary for seniors in high school to have a Senior Skip Day at the class's discretion. About 3 weeks before graduation, we had spent the first couple hours of school one day at the town hall practicing for our senior class play. (We had no school auditorium.) Our class was so small that the whole class had to participate to have a play. At the end of play practice, we decided that day would be our skip day. I had a car, so I talked to my friend Jim Plathe and we invited the two best-looking girls in the class to come along; we went for a drive in the country. After an hour or two, we came across some pheasants. As in our family hunts, I got out the rifle and shot a nice plump cock. We discussed what to do.

We went to Cousin Marie Kanthak's house, near where we were, and borrowed flour and lard. There was a nice grassy place along the creek in the Kanthak pasture, so we went there to cook and eat lunch. All my possessions were in my car trunk, including an old frying pan. (My folks had moved to St. Cloud and I stayed behind to finish out my last few months of high school, so there was a lot of stuff in my trunk!) We built a fire, the young ladies helped cook the pheasant, and we all ate it.

Another "hunting" adventure was that even when my brother Ralph was still in high school, he never went hunting. But on Sunday afternoons, we would haul the family chopping block from the woodpile out into the plowed field north of our place, pound two large spikes a little way into it, and use the nail heads as targets. We would alternate shooting. The winner was the one whose nail was driven in the most. Ralph seemed to always win. Six months before December 7th, Pearl Harbor Day, Ralph was drafted into the Army. In training, his superiors eventually assigned him a gun. Then came target shooting. He kept putting the bullet in the center of the target, so in a few days, he was helping the other recruits learn to shoot. Eventually, he earned a sharpshooter medal. Ralph was home on leave a year later, and we were driving around doing some shooting at a merganser (a type of large duck) wheeling above a slough hole—a "small pond" in Eastern Shore jargon—and on the fourth shot, he knocked it down from flight. My thoughts: WWII, Germans, beware. You know...like the Sergeant York movie about a sharpshooter in the First World War!

As mentioned before, a regular Sunday afternoon adventure was that my dad and I would go pheasant hunting. By the time I was about 14, I had borrowed a double-barreled shotgun from Uncle Wilbert. It had been hanging on a nail on an open porch at the Hackert farm for several years, so of course it was very rusty. The first thing I had to do was to take emery cloth and get rid of the rust. One firing pin was missing, so I took a nail about the right diameter, cut it the right length, and filed it to fit (mostly). It blew back a little bit when I fired the gun, so it was my custom when I shot to close my eyes. I had eyeglasses, so that helped too.

After I had used that double-barreled shotgun a bit, I told Dad when we hunted together that the chokes were gone, so it gave a broad shot pattern. I do not remember ever getting a bird with that gun, but only when hunting alone with Dad's gun. But using my double barrel shotgun was more fun than firing off firecrackers on the Fourth of July!

With Dad's gun, though, I shot many pheasants. Whenever I'd go out before supper for 30 to 45 minutes, I'd come home with three cock pheasants.

Another hunting/shooting story—My dad John had moved to St. Cloud and they had a Thanksgiving shooting contest like you see in Western movies. The prize was a turkey. Of course, my dad John stayed through the many levels of competition and finally won the turkey. It was the challenge of the game and not the turkey that he enjoyed. After all, he had scads of turkeys at the grocery store for his customers to buy for their Thanksgiving dinner.

Another story is that my dad and I went out hunting on a Sunday afternoon and hunted east of town. (None of my brothers or sisters were interested in hunting.) We came across my classmate, Jim Plathe, and his dad out hunting in the same area. Jim and I went to school together from the second grade through high school and then to St. John's University. So the two fathers and two sons hunted together for several hours, telling stories, shooting, and making general conversation.

One of the stories from Jim's dad was that he bet his neighbor that if he carried one of the neighbor's pigs when it was 1 year old, from the neighbor's pig barn to his yard, he would own the pig. If not, he would pay the neighbor $35. And he won! The trick was that he would carry the pig that distance once or twice a week, so both he and the pig got used to the carrying. Good exercise and good pork ribs!

Besides father-and-son hunting with my dad, we often did things together. Maybe this was because my brother Don was away at college, and my oldest brother Ralph was in the Army, so I was the only son at home. Even in my earlier days, though, my dad and I did things together.

When I was about 8 years old, occasionally I would go with my dad to pick up the mail. In Bellingham, there was no mail delivery in town. Since it was too small (population of about 200), the train would drop off the mail sacks at about 1 PM. If business was slow, Dad would walk to the post office, about three blocks away, to get the mail out of the post office box. Sometimes when available, I would go along. If there was no action at work and some relative or friend was around, we would stop by for a beer for Dad and a root beer for me. Our county, Lac qui Parle, was dry, so only 3.2 beer was available. It was beer, but even a kid had to drink three or four glasses to even feel a little buzz.

In my teens, we would go shopping to Madison, Minnesota (ten miles away) for groceries or hardware, and usually would end the trip with soda or ice cream. By doing this during sales in a big-store grocery like IGA, Mom could save dollars on groceries.

After we moved to St. Cloud, I lived at home the last 3 years I attended St. John's. Many evenings when my homework was done, I would go to Dad's grocery store at quitting time. After he finished checking out and putting stuff away, we would go out to a bar for a drink before bedtime. The St. Cloud Hotel was a favorite place. Dad's drink beyond beer was Old Grand-dad Bourbon, which I developed a taste for too. Another place we went was Sonny Stolpmann's bar across the street from the St. Cloud Library.

When I was younger, Sonny was in the band at my high school. He would come to our house after school for supper since he had to be back in town that evening to play in the band for a basketball game. He was not a relative but was related to my dad's uncle, John Stolpmann. I heard a few years after I left Minnesota that Sonny had died of a heart attack; he complained about not feeling very well, and when his wife called to have him come to dinner, she discovered that he had died.

In later years, after I married and would come to visit, my dad and I would continue to go out for a drink and family discussion. In a way, this continues in my generation. My son Eric comes to visit one or two weekends after Labor Day and we go to a Delaware state park beach for a couple of hours to discuss the young ladies swimming, politics, and family issues. Usually Eric goes for a swim, although I gave that up a few years ago. When my son Mike comes to visit, usually a trip to the Ocean City Boardwalk is in order. He is the runner; I do maybe a mile, while he does 3 to 5 miles. Of course, we talk about his life issues and, again, politics, investing, and science stuff. (He has an interest in the science of light just as his dad does.)

❧ Chapter 17 ❧

Generous John

Let me add an introduction to these stories about my dad John. He was a very modest person, not flamboyant. He believed in the words of the Bible. When doing good or trying to be helpful to others, he followed the saying, "Do not let your left hand know what your right hand is doing." He probably learned that from his father, Grandpa Peter; years later I heard about Peter helping others in times of problems in their lives, in stories from my cousins and other relatives. I am including this section to encourage others to be generous.

When we lived in St. Cloud, Dad ran a neighborhood grocery store. Periodically, Dad would have me take food to the "Poor Clares," a contemplative group of Catholic sisters. This would happen particularly during seasonal celebrations like Christmas and Easter.

Another example of his generosity was that while I went to St. John's, I was asked by a Benedictine monk to get my dad's suggestion on something they could send to Benedictine missionaries in Africa that was stable enough to send in the mail. Dad suggested that one of the things that would be a real present was a stick of summer sausage. Then they ordered some, but Dad refused payment. This was his contribution to the missionary effort.

In later life, I heard from my dad's cousin (who was my age) that Grandpa Peter was that way, too. Relatives in North Dakota had a house fire, and the house and everything was lost. Grandpa Peter got together tables and chairs, beds, sheets, towels, and more, loaded it all on his farm truck, and had one of his sons deliver it to the relatives to help them over their disaster.

Another story of John that I've told you before happened in the store. A little 4-year-old was sent by her mother (four doors from the store) with a list of groceries to get, along with the money for them, plus a few pennies for the little one to pick out a piece of candy for herself. The child spent maybe 15 minutes deciding what she wanted, then negotiated with my dad on the price. She had maybe 3 cents, but wanted a 5- or 6-cent item. Finally, my dad yielded and explained to her that the candy was going to be a sale item that Saturday, so he would sell it to her for the sale price. Twenty years later, the little girl, now a grown woman, came by with her two little girls. She drove 50 miles out of the way on their trip, to see Mr. Hackert, the man who was her friend when she was only a little girl, and to visit with this very kind man she had told her kids about.

My dad did a substantial part of his grocery business on credit. This had been his policy when we lived in Bellingham and Dad was the manager of the grain elevator. Typically, whether I was 6 years old or 14 years old, if my mother needed something like flour or yeast, one of us kids was sent to the store. The sale was recorded, and at the end of the month, my dad wrote the grocer a check. My dad did that later, when he became the grocer.

He also delivered orders he got over the phone. For instance, he would make deliveries on Tuesdays and Fridays. As the boss, he had two or three clerks to help out when he was out on deliveries. This way he kept in touch personally with his customers. Also, a lot of customers were older people and could not get out to do their shopping. And many customers were wives and mothers with little children, and no extra car to go shopping. (The dad had the family car to go to work.) My opinion is that Dad considered his grocery-delivering as a job of charity. He would, as much as possible, visit with the customer, at least the housebound, as often as time allowed, and probably more if there was a problem to discuss. In later years, the old 1937 Ford died when he talked too long to a housebound older lady, and this idling car waiting for his return overheated. He said that as he came out to the car after that delivery, the car engine was in its death throes, screeching to a stop. But it had served through the years as the store truck, and earlier it had faithfully run through the years in Bellingham as the "tractor," hauling hay and feed for the dairy cows, preparing a garden to plant potatoes, and completing so many other farm jobs. It surely had over 200,000 miles of hard service.

Another way my dad John was generous with his time—Grandpa Voigt and Grandma Mary were getting on in years when we moved to St. Cloud in 1945. As I said before, being a good son-in-law, John would go over to their house mainly in winter, but also when needed in spring and fall. He would get up early in the morning, drive over there (about 10 or 15 blocks), charge the furnace stoker with fuel, adjust the heating system, and then head back home for breakfast and to work at the grocery store by 8 AM. This went on for at least the 4 years I went to St. John's.

I sorta got chosen for the "Help-Grandpa-and-Grandma" effort too. I usually had an 8 AM class, 12 miles away by bus or car, but I pitched in when it was necessary. For example, in the fall and spring, their big house had storm windows and screens to change. It was a full two-story brick house, so the job involved a ladder to change the window stuff. I was aware of houses with changeable storm windows and screens ever since I was old enough to help in Bellingham. That was my job there.

Another job that was fun for me—Grandpa's 1936 Ford V8 coupe had stopped running for several weeks during the cold weather in the fall. All it needed was for someone to clean the spark plugs and gap them, replace the point set in the distributor, adjust the timing, and away it went. In retrospect, that would have been a much better car than my 1937 Ford; I should have offered to buy it when Grandpa couldn't drive anymore and I was still in graduate school in Detroit.

A similar thing happened a number of years later when our kids were teenagers and younger. Miss Edna, who lived next door, had a 1962 Chevy II, and the neighbor on the opposite side (a mechanic) looked after her car in her old age. Surprise—one morning in the middle of his life, he "bought the farm"—he died suddenly. So that car became my toy to play with on Saturday afternoons, as needed. Soon Miss Edna died, so the family said I should buy it. This was our first "second" car. It ran for another 130,000 miles: It went to Ray to go to work; to my son Mike to use to go to California for work and graduate school; back to Ray for an extra car for kids in high school; and finally, it was sold to a friend to race locally on Saturday afternoons.

Chapter 18

John – Recreation, Activity, Adventure

In the Peter Hackert family, most were bilingual and some trilingual. Soon after Grandma Martha died, Grandpa Peter married Grandma Ida. Grandma Ida only spoke High (or classical) German, but Grandpa Peter spoke Low German (as his first language), and both High German and English. This was necessary since the family lived among other German immigrants who also spoke three languages. It was the custom in the family that Grandma Ida only spoke High German and English to her daughters. Grandpa Peter spoke all three languages to his offspring, but mainly talked Low German to his sons. So imagine the whole group around the supper table, including the local country schoolteacher. She was there since the school was across the road from the farmhouse, so during school the teacher lived at the Hackert house. If John asked the teacher to pass the potatoes, he spoke English (her only language). If Grandma Ida asked her daughter to pass the potatoes, it was in High German. If Grandpa Peter asked a son to pass the potatoes, it was in Low German. They all knew what language to speak to one or the other, even when the kids were very little. Just imagine 12 people all talking about all kinds of things in three languages!

My dad told me this story – When John's brother Wilbert was 4 years old, he was robed in coats, mittens, and cap, and went with Grandpa Peter on the seat of a horse-drawn wagon to do the shopping in Rosen, Minnesota, on a snowy, windy winter morning. As they passed the second farmplace grove of trees, a dog came out and started barking at the horses. That went on for maybe 10 minutes with Grandpa hollering at the dog, and it finally tired and went back to its farmplace. After maybe another 10 minutes went by, Wilbert questioned, "Pa, how did you know that was a boy dog?" (since his dad had hollered in Low German, the language of the males of the family).

I may have mentioned this before, but when John was about 10 or 12, he was out hunting when a great thunderstorm came up. He was on the far side of Yellow Bank River from the house, so he had to go by way of the bridge to get home. When he got there, the bridge was under water, but he decided to cross by wading through the raging torrent. Obviously, he survived, and his gun was not lost—a very exciting adventure for quite a young kid.

When my dad was a young man, it was the custom to go to public dances (since there was no radio or TV). By the time 1920 was approaching, he was of the opinion that cars were a step backward. How come? Later in life, he explained this to me. Imagine him going to the dance in a buggy with a team of horses and meeting a nice girl who agreed that John would take her home afterward. The horses knew the way, so the driver (John) had his hands free to discuss life with his new friend all the way to her home. (Psychosocially, this was regarded as the early stages of courting.) With a car, one would have to keep at least one hand on the steering wheel.

After we moved to Bellingham, in the 1930s and 1940s my mom and dad went to dances usually once or twice a week. In those days, the Ben Kelzers were good friends. I found it fascinating that Ben could tell stories for 2 hours, never repeating one, and many of the stories were humorous, and none were derogatory about people in general, and about women in particular. One of his sayings, for example, was when they were visiting us at Christmastime. My brother Don got a collar for his dog, a stray that had befriended him. Ben's comment was "That was a three-dollar collar for a one-and-a-half-dollar dog." I often thought that Ben could have had a radio program where he would tell his stories.

After we moved to Minnesota (when I was 5 years old), I realized we had scads of relatives, and our family visited them and they visited us often. There was a pattern—old people's birthdays were celebrated; also, it seemed like every uncle and aunt, and also grandpas and grandmas celebrated the Christmas holiday, and almost every evening we had parties to attend with the whole clan. Typically, we would go to Grandpa Peter's house for an evening, and since all the farmers were in the dairy business, the party would start about 9 PM. The "old" men would play cards. The young people would go into the attic, and older ones would tell ghost stories to frighten the little ones. On a clear moonlit night, the kids would go sledding and tobogganing on the hills along the creek. Later in the evening, Grandma Ida would have prepared ice cream mix; some of the men had brought some ice out of the farm's icehouse, and the cousins my age took turns cranking the ice cream churns. Those that cranked got to lick the agitators when the ice cream was done. Finally, around 11:30 PM, all had a good lunch of hotdishes, cake, and the ice cream. There was no eating after midnight since, if it was Saturday night, people had to fast from midnight if they were going to Mass and Communion the next day. (I wondered if that's why on Christmas there was Midnight Mass; for once, there was no fasting before midnight for Mass and Communion.) One favorite place for this kind of party was at Great-Uncle and Aunt Volkenant's. My aunt made a fancy cake where the piece of cake was coated with crushed peanuts. Aunt Mary Spors's prize dessert was cream puffs. I still wonder how the whipped cream got inside!

Often in the 1930s, after Dad was home from work and supper was over, we would go for a short visit to Grandpa Peter's. I remember one time when my mother, who was a persnickety housekeeper, announced as we finished supper that we would just get up from the table, no washing dishes or cleanup, and leave abruptly to visit Grandpa's.

Around about 1940, Grandpa and Grandma had moved to Nassau, Minnesota, and it was decided they needed a new roof. All the uncles and aunts and cousins showed up, and the older men did the roof while the older kids did stuff like moving shingles up ladders. I was one for that job. Of course, the ladies had brought scads of food, particularly

Minnesota hotdishes (mostly German food), so everyone was well fed. Littler ones were water boys and girls. The job got done in one short day. The farmers had to fit it in between morning and evening milking times.

In later years, I was visiting my dad in St. Cloud and we went to the Grandpa Peter farm, and my dad spent several hours going around, telling me when buildings were built, and about problems around the farm. For example, a water piping system had been built from the windmill to the pig barn. At one time the pipes leaked, and that left a hole in the yard along the way. It was dug up and repaired, and then the hole was filled in.

Below the bridge adjacent to the Hackert farm was a deep pool caused by fast running water in heavy rains. It was known as the Peter Hackert swimming hole. On a hot summer Sunday afternoon, when my dad and his relatives were visiting together, it was a usual thing to go down to the swimming hole for a swim to cool off. The tradition around Bellingham on a summer night at full moon was to go for a swim. Apparently, the high school boys and girls would go there, usually skinny-dipping.

My dad and mom and family usually went on vacation trips. In about 1934, we went to visit Grandma Martha's relatives near Tomah, Wisconsin. We still had the 1928 Pontiac, so my dad fitted the rack to the rear of the car and added the trunk, where we had all our clothes and stuff. There was no room for it inside the car. When we got to the Semrau farm, I was impressed by several young guys, John's cousins who were already mostly bald at only 21 to 25 years old. That's where the baldness in the Hackert clan came from. In comparison, Grandpa Peter had a beard and mustache and a full head of hair. At that age, I thought, poor Grandma Ida. Just imagine when they went off to bed and Grandma had to put up with his bristly, wiry facial hair. Later in life, I figured all that wiry hair probably turned Grandma on.

In Wisconsin, I got to see and go into my first train tunnel. (We lived on the open prairie.) We also picked berries that were in season and visited and saw Indian markets and their touristy wares, like baskets.

One day we saw the famous train, the 400 (later renamed the Twin Cities 400) go by at more than 60 miles per hour. It was said that it was called the 400 because it took 400 minutes to go from Minneapolis to Chicago. We visited Semrau relatives who had a dry goods store in Tomah. That was where my dad John got it in his head to be a storekeeper, not a farmer. Of course, he did that (sort of) in the grain elevator, and then in the grocery store. Over later years, I would stop in to see the relatives in Tomah when I could.

In 1938, we had a new car, a 1937 Ford, and went on a vacation trip back to Anamoose, North Dakota. We took two Benedictine sisters who taught in the Rosen Catholic grade school to their motherhouse in Moorhead, Minnesota. One of the sisters was Sister Philip, who was my teacher in first grade. If you did something really bad, you got sent to the principal (and also eighth grade teacher), Sister Borger.

After stopping at Moorhead, we went on to Anamoose and stayed mostly with the Rudnick family on the farm, but visited other friends in the area. The Rudnick family had about five kids in a new house, and son Lawrence, who was about 2 years older than me, was the one I mostly played with. He had built a windmill rig and was trying to generate electricity, with no success. We tried a number of things (I was 11, he was 13) but nothing worked. When I was in high school physics class later, I found out it was very simple; a conductive wire like copper moving through a magnetic field caused electricity to flow. Later I realized I should have asked Uncle Wilbert, my dad John's brother; he had set up a functioning windmill on Grandpa Peter's farm, and wired the house for 35-volt electric service. For several years in that timeframe, the Hackerts had electric lights on the farm while other farmers still used kerosene lamps.

After visiting around Anamoose, we went to Winnipeg, Manitoba, to visit Mom's Uncle Kraemer. He ran a shoe manufacturing company, and we had a tour of the factory and learned a lot about how shoes were made commercially. Another big deal during that visit was a restaurant dinner in Winnipeg that cost about 40 cents a meal, including a meat, two vegetables, and pie for dessert.

An important thing I learned was that the USA money was more valuable than that of Canada, and one could buy a complete dinner with dessert and drinks for about 32 cents, much cheaper than at home. Later in life, I went to graduate school in Detroit, and when finances were low and I had time, I would go over to Windsor, Ontario in Canada, across the Detroit River, for a good meal—cheap, even counting bus fare.

In 1939, we went on the once-in-a-lifetime trip to New York to visit John's older brother Frank in Whitestone, NY, and to attend the World's Fair. At that time, besides spending a number of days at the fair, my cousin Jerry and I walked over to a nearby bridge being built, the Whitestone/Bronx Bridge. We also walked to the Whitestone Airport (a small one) to see planes coming and going, and to talk about being pilots. After World War II, Jerry joined the Air Force and was the third man in a B-52, doing most of the other stuff like dropping bombs and taking anti-air attack measures. While we were in New York, Lou Gehrig gave up baseball because of a strange disease he had.

While we were away from Minnesota, my two youngest sisters stayed on the Hackert farm with Uncle Wilbert. They saw a tornado come by that wiped out a farmhouse, but no one was killed. (All were safely in a strong basement.) After arriving home, we went to see the place. Imagine the force of the storm—pieces of straw were driven like nails into the remains of a hardwood floor left over the basement. Our area around Bellingham was a tornado alley, and also had high winds caused by cyclones. My dad John and our family would go out on a Sunday to see the destruction, and Dad would take pictures. He was a persistent photographer, not only for family occasions like First Communion.

Another family story happened at Rosen in that period. A group of farmers was playing cards in the store on the west end of Rosen, on an evening after the day's work was done. The storekeeper finally asked them to leave, since it was closing time. One fellow went and got a loaf of bread, and went to pay for it with a $1000 bill. The storekeeper did not have change. Uncle Jack Spors spoke up, he pulled out a roll of big bills, and he made change for the $1000 bill—one-upmanship.

I learned later that he had a couple of grain trucks and did a little grain buying and selling and hauling. In that business, the operator had to do cash business. Like my dad, he would not deal with a check from some stranger coming off the road with his truck and wanting to buy a truckload of wheat, for example, for several hundred dollars. Also, I knew from my dad that Dad was bonded for up to $40,000, since he had papers as a legal weighmaster and grain buyer. He often shipped railroad cars of grain worth many thousands of dollars. Not only did the elevator have scales for buying and selling grain, but also had automated weighing of grain going into a railroad car to ship to the Minneapolis Grain Exchange.

Besides being a very outgoing couple, my dad and mom often had guests at our house and visited their many relatives and friends. My parents were very much into going out to dances, both public and private. I learned this after we moved to Minnesota. Usually they went out with friends, leaving about 9 PM and returning about midnight. Dances usually started about 9 PM; this was necessary, at least in a farming community where most farmers had milking chores in the early evening.

So in my early years in Bellingham, what did the Hackert kids do when the parents left for the evening? The older ones would wake us younger ones up. (It was after our bedtime when our parents left.) We would remove the kitchen table plasticized tablecloth and get out candy-making stuff, after deciding among us what candy to make. When it was done and it was winter, the candy was put outside to cool and set. Then the question was where to store it. The conclusion was that Mom would find it, so we had to destroy the evidence: Eat it. That worked, since we six kids could eat it easily. Then before midnight, all physical evidence had to be restored to its pre-9 PM state. We had to make sure the sugar

90

can was still as full as before by moving some from the open sugar bag to the sugar can, for example.

During the latter part of our stay in Bellingham, the Ben Kelzers were close family friends. Many times, Dad, Mom, Ben Kelzer, and his wife would go to a dance once or twice a week. In the Minnesota area, if someone got married, the custom was that they would have a wedding dance often open to friends and relatives. I am sure that a lot of dances my parents attended were wedding dances. This went on around Bellingham while I was growing up, but also around St. Cloud. Even at the grocery store, Dad had many customers and Mom had many relatives and church friends, many of whom had noontime dinner parties that included dances, for all kinds of occasions.

JOHN AND HALLOWEEN

When I was a kid, my dad told stories about Halloween in his youth. Was he involved? I do not know (but probably, sometimes). He always told them as local stories.

It was Halloween and the guys decided to visit the elderly farmer who lived alone. Late in the evening, when all was quiet, they went to the farmer's place and went to work on his buggy (no cars then). In those days, this farmer's habit was to come to town several times a week to buy things at the store. They removed the wheels from the buggy, large ones on the back and smaller ones in front. They put the wheels back on, with the front ones moved to the back and the back to the front. For the next week or two, as usual, the farmer came to town, and people laughed as he went by. With the wheels reversed, it looked like he was going uphill all the time. Eventually someone told him, and his buggy was put back to normal.

On another occasion, another old farmer had declared that nobody was going to do any pranks on him. He sat in front of his barn with a lantern lit, holding a shotgun. He eventually fell asleep and the guys took over. They took his buggy apart, got ladders, and piece by piece hauled the parts on top of the barn and reassembled it. When the sun came up, the farmer awoke to see his buggy on top of the barn.

In 1987, Bellingham, Minnesota had a 100-year anniversary. My wife and I, my sister Rusty, and my parents, John and Marie, attended. In talking to my Uncle Anton and Aunt Elizabeth (Dad's sister), I heard this story of a Bellingham Halloween. Apparently the young guys, and some not so young, had borrowed the cow of a widow who lived near the town's water tower. They walked it across town, up the hill, and into the school, and tied it in the school superintendent's office at the end of the upstairs hall. But I told Anton that was not all the story. I had firm orders that I could not go Halloweening from my parents. When I got to school in the morning, my homeroom was next to the office. The cow had diarrhea during the night, and the office floor was hardwood, so the poor cow slipped in its poop and finally lay there in the stinking mess in the morning. I was accused of being one of the bad ones, but my dad John, my mom Marie, and five brothers and sisters were witnesses attesting that I had been home all evening and night.

On another Halloween night, I was out with the guys, along with not so young town and farm guys. Someone had gotten a flatbed two-wheel trailer. We had gotten the school superintendent's outhouse almost up on the trailer when (praise God) the back door of the house opened and (behold) there stood the superintendent, backlit in his nightshirt, bare ankles and feet showing. He hollered that we should be careful and not let it drop—somebody might get hurt! He announced that earlier in the day he had already hired the drayman to come tomorrow to remove that thing from the front steps of the school (where the guys had planned to take it) and put it back on its foundation in his backyard. (In those days, most people in our town had outhouses.)

Chapter 19

John the Innovator and Craftsman

When we got the dairy herd to supply bottled milk for the town of Bellingham, we had to modify our barn for the cows. The first task was to install a stanchion for each cow. The next was to build gutters. This meant building cement forms, getting gravel to mix and pour cement, and letting it cure. Dad knew how to do all that stuff, probably having done it when he was young helping out on the farm. With cold winters, the cows had to spend most of the time in the barn. To start with, we had two cows and bought six more. Later, when the milk business was getting better, we bought more cows.

At first, the cows were only on one side of the barn, but as the business expanded, the other side formerly used for chickens was also changed to a cow parlor. My dad figured out a water system for the cows. At each stall was a water bowl (from Sears Roebuck) piped up to a 55-gallon tank. Water was pumped at the well into garbage cans on a flat, low-bed cart. This was wheeled to the barn, and transferred to the tank in the barn one bucketful at a time. This was done from a raised deck via a funnel attached to the side of the barn. The funnel allowed water brought to the deck on the outside of the wall to flow through the wall to the tank on the inside of the same wall. It was necessary to have the tank raised so the tank water flowed by gravity to each drinking bowl at each stall. Each cow could then turn on the water to fill her bowl by using her nose to press on a lever in her bowl that opened the valve and let the water run into it. Usually water handling was done about twice a day.

The barn was fairly tight, and without heating, it kept reasonably warm inside. As I remember, usually two or three times a winter the water pipes froze, when it was 20 to 25 degrees below zero. To fix this, we wrapped some old cloths around the frozen pipes and poured boiling water over the rags. This was typically an extra 20-minute interruption in daily chores. We bought alfalfa hay, normally by the stack. Of course, a twice-a-day chore was to throw down hay from the hayloft and fill the mangers so the cows could eat the alfalfa.

Imagine how simple caring for the cattle was in summer! One would call them in from the pasture, close each in its stanchion in the barn, and milk them. We never got around to milking by machine, only by hand. The milking crew was Mom and me. During the first winter, Dad built a corn stalk feeder in the barnyard. Of course, then I could haul purchased corn stalks as well as the alfalfa hay. The corn stalk bundles were stacked first outside the barnyard so one could get on the corn stack and pitch a supply for the cows into the feeder in the barnyard. For several years, the Menzel farm adjacent to our property had a crop of corn. After corn picking was done, I would herd the cattle into the field for an hour or two when I had time, so that instead of feeding them corn stalks in a feeder, they could eat them directly from the field. Also, sometimes kids from town were hired to do the herding.

We had an outside entrance to the cellar and had milk-handling equipment there. The milk processing was mostly done by my sisters and mom. The milk would be cooled with cold water from the well, filtered, mixed to blend rich Guernsey milk with less rich Holstein milk, and then bottled. Most of the time, my sisters delivered the milk, collected payment for it, and kept the accounts. This was good experience for my sister Katie, who later worked with Dad in the grocery store when the family moved to St. Cloud. I remember an incident when it was at least 30 degrees below zero, so I helped deliver the milk. Moisture from my exhaled breath would form frost on my eyelashes, and eventually my eyes would freeze shut. I stopped, took off a glove, and thawed my eye by putting my warm hand over my eye. By then, my fingers started to freeze—on with the glove and back to delivering for several minutes, till the cycle started again.

The bottled milk was delivered in a handcart built by my dad. He bought two bicycle wheels, axles, and other hardware from the Sears catalog. The cart box was designed so that a set of milk bottle hand-carried wire baskets fit snugly in the cart box. The cart was balanced so when my sisters delivered milk, they did not have to lift the weight, but just push it along. Pneumatic tires on the cart rolled fairly evenly over rough gravel.

My dad and I would go out on a Sunday afternoon and look to buy hay. We would buy it by the ton or the stack, but most farmers preferred to sell by the stack. That way, with good judgment by my dad, we usually did better dollar-wise. I drove the car then and could borrow a four-wheel trailer fitted with a hayrack. I always ran the load through the scales at the elevator to see the tonnage we were using for the cattle being fed. A typical run to get hay in winter was to drive the car and hayrack to the snow-covered field. Then I jacked up each of the back wheels (drive wheels), and put on a car chain that could cover each tire. I drove the car and empty rack through the snow to the haystack and out to the road, maybe three times, to make a good track through the snow. (I did not want to get stuck in the snow with a load on—and I never did.) When I would first open a new stack, I'd remove the "roof" of hay which had been rained on and had deteriorated. Then I would use a pitchfork to load about a ton of hay. I would then drive the load out to the road, remove the chains, and go maybe 2 to 8 miles on the snowy roads to the elevator to weigh it and to the barn to unload it. (I wouldn't want to use the chains any more than necessary, to keep them from breaking and damaging the car.) The old faithful '37 Ford did that, even though the engine sometimes got so hot that the vent on the top of the engine had "smoke" pouring out. That meant that, coming up to the barn, I had to hang my head out the window to see where I was going. It was a wonder the poor abused 1937 Ford kept going (and for years later).

For summer cattle feed, we rented 30 acres of pasture next to our property. Of course Dad knew all about fences and gates so he decided on the proper places for gates in the fence between properties, and we built them. I had a summer chore to borrow a team of horses and a hay mower to cut the weeds in the pasture. We did not want the cattle eating weeds, as that could cause bad tasting milk.

Along with the 30-acre pasture came a fairly big garden and an apple orchard. We planted potatoes in the garden, enough to last most of the year. To prepare the garden, we plowed it with a borrowed team of horses and a plow. The garden plot needed to be pulverized, so Dad built a drag made with two-by-fours nailed together for a crude platform, with many big spikes (nails) sticking out of the bottom. I used the car to drag that back and forth across the garden to break up the soil. We planted the potatoes, harvested them by hand, and stored them in bins in the cellar.

For the apple orchard, I picked apples and Mom made pies and applesauce canned in fruit jars. We only used about 10 percent of the apples, so later in the season, when the apples fell to the ground, I shoveled them onto a trailer, drove from the orchard to the barn, piled them next to the pig pen, and fed the apples to the pigs. The idea is to use everything you have and convert it to profit. Feed pigs apples, and avoid buying some oats and corn to feed them. Dad, who was raised on a self-sufficient farm, carried over his experiences from growing up, and used what he learned to help in many ways as described above.

We also raised chickens; that was mom's pet project. We would buy chicks in the spring and mainly raise them for eating as soon as they had grown enough, which usually was in the early fall. Of course, this was a cash crop. But we sometimes kept a limited number of chickens for eggs during the winter. We found out that having chickens for eggs was more productive if the chickens had light for about 12 hours instead of depending on daylight in the short days of winter. My dad built a timer to turn on the light at about 4 AM. He built it around an old wind-up alarm clock. It worked by winding a string on a spool when the alarm went off. The string pulled a board set in such a way that it worked as a clapper and turned on the light switch. Of course, the clock's alarm had to be wound and reset each day, but that was better than for someone to set an alarm, get out of bed, and go turn on the lights in the chicken house at 4 AM.

At one time, we were only keeping a hundred selected laying hens. We usually got about 90 eggs per day, but when it sometimes dropped down, I was asked to find out which chickens were slackers. There was nothing that we knew of to get a chicken to resume laying eggs, but the slacker went into the Sunday dinner pot; we could not afford to buy feed for a non-producing chicken. Finding the slacker was not too difficult. Each chicken would usually have a preferred nest, so it would be identified as laying eggs or not.

In the grain business, often when the weather was not quite right, grain would arrive to be bought, but it was too wet. Wet grain cannot be stored safely since it will start to ferment in the elevator storage bin. In the early days, that judgment was the responsibility of my dad, the elevator manager. It was a sad day if a farmer came in with his harvested grain and had to be turned away. From my earliest years, I saw my dad doing grain moisture analysis using a heating-in-oil method, distilling the water off from a measured sample and measuring it in a marked glass tube. This was a chore that went along with many other parts of the job, like buying and selling grain, loading railroad cars to ship and sell grain, operating a commercial grain cleaner to remove weed seeds from the grain, mixing several grains for hog or chicken feed, and grinding a mix to the customers' needs (busy, busy guy).

About 1942, the technology of moisture measurement in grain developed to almost instant measurement. Instead of getting four moisture results in an 8- to 10-hour workday, the test took only seconds. A load of grain would arrive, and before unloading, one could take a thief sample, probing with a hollow tube sampler at various parts of the load, mix the sample, add about 3 ounces to the electronic analyzer, press some button, and have an answer. If the grain was too wet, it was rejected; those days were before commercial hot air grain dryers.

Another technology that dad introduced was a barley pearler. This removed the hard skin of the kernel, and one could grade the barley by its color. One year during harvest time, a number of farmers from an area near Bellingham delivered barley to the elevator that was good quality malting barley. Separating that from barley for eating or for animal feed, Dad shipped several railroad cars of malting barley to the Minneapolis market and got a premium for it. The elevator was a co-op, so he kept track of who delivered it to the elevator and how much each one delivered. These farmers got a bonus payment for their premium barley. (This required much recording and paperwork, but that was Dad's job; he treated people right and they remained loyal customer-owners of the business.)

When I worked for Del Monte Company I was the plant corn chemist and did corn moisture measurement. At first, this involved a xylene distillation method that was quite tedious. Eventually we changed to an electronic method as my dad had done in the elevator. Moisture in sweet corn is very important; it is a measure of sweetness—the corn is at its peak sweetness at maximum moisture content. Beyond that point, the sugar (sweetness) starts changing to starch (non-sweet starchiness).

A game my dad and I played went like this: Mom was all set to get bushes to put alongside the wash lines. My dad was against it, but he finally agreed to do it. When Mom's friend brought the bushes to our house, Dad told me to go dig the six holes, but to make them about one-third deeper than needed, then fill in the bottom third with raw manure from the manure pile, and then plant the bushes. The idea was that the raw manure would kill the bushes, Mom would have had her way, but the plants would die. Lo and behold, the bushes thrived even more so than her friend's bushes! Unintended consequences!

When my youngest daughter Carol was at the learning-to-walk age, she did not appear to have enough self-confidence to do it. We were visiting my mom's parents, and Dad and I were at a park with Carol. After a while, my dad suggested he would get her to walk alone. He separated us about 15 feet, gave Carol a clothespin for her to clutch in each hand, and pushed her off by herself. I could see the whiteness of her fingers as she clutched the clothespins, but she walked alone. That demonstrated to her she could do it, and shortly she was walking around, and soon after that the clothespins were not needed.

Another craftsman skill was John's wallpapering. Over the years while I was growing up, we always lived in a rental house. It was the custom that the renter could do what he wished as far as the inside of the house was concerned, particularly with respect to the inside walls and woodwork. My mother was the painter. As I said before, at 5 years old, I remember moving into the house across the road from the grain elevator where my dad was manager. My mother loathed the color of the inside woodworks, so for days before we moved in (we lived temporarily in a house about the middle of town), my mother painted the woodwork the color she chose.

I was given the job to rock the baby buggy to keep my brand-new sister Lucille from screaming and hollering. Of course, my mother took care of the baby essentials like nursing and changing diapers.

After we moved in, mother was not satisfied with the wallpaper, so my dad had the job of applying new wallpaper on evenings and weekends. He appeared to be an expert at it, probably doing that in the new house at his home on the farm. I was fascinated at his mixing paste to stick the paper on the wall. He could also "paint" the paste on the back side of a single sheet of wallpaper, then fold it expertly so no front side of the paper got paste on it. Then he started sticking it on the wall, first at the ceiling, then down to the bottom of the wall, getting each narrow sheet exactly straight, and one narrow row exactly overlapping the next row, so the pattern grew as he papered across the wall. As each piece of paper was attached to the wall, he had a wide brush to get the paper firmly stuck on the wall. When done, the repeating pattern all along the wall looked perfectly symmetrical.

My dad also had two relatives in the family, contractors who did wallpapering along with building houses, building additions, and remodeling kitchens. They were my Uncle Edwin, the former Peavey Elevator manager in the 1920s, and my Uncle Alvin.

❧ Chapter 20 ❧

John the Miller

As I said before, the main job my dad John had as elevator manager in Bellingham was buying and selling grain. But a secondary job as part of the elevator work was operating a mill where farmers brought their own grain or bought some, and had it ground/milled as they specified (coarse to fine).

The mill consisted of two steel wheels. Each wheel was made of a horizontal shaft about the thickness of a sturdy man's upper arm and about 4 to 6 feet long, with a disk-shaped vertical end plate perpendicular at one end. Imagine these two grinding assemblies each looked like a monstrous wheel-and-axle for a wagon or car, or like a tremendous nail/spike with a head and shaft. At the shaft-end of the grinding assembly was a 230-volt electric motor, which spun its side of the unit during milling. Each plate was about 4 feet in diameter and about 8 inches thick. All this was made out of a single piece of metal. The two vertical end plates faced each other and rotated in opposite directions to maximize grinding. On the inner surface of each vertical wheel were bolted about eight grinder plates to cover about two-thirds of the outside face of the end plate, making concentric circles. And all the parts that I've described, all the ones that spin and grind, are in an enclosure made of heavy steel so you cannot see the parts, you can only hear them doing their job.

There were controls to move the plates closer or farther apart. When milling fine, the plates would be adjusted so they were as close together as possible, but not touching. To grind coarser, the two plates were moved apart, usually to the coarseness of the ground feed the customer wanted. The grain flowed out of a bin above the mill, down a chute, and, fed by gravity, into the space between the two closely rotating plates. It then dropped out of the mill to be conveyed to a truck or trailer grain box, or to a sack-filling station in the mill room, if the farmer wanted to handle the ground feed by hand in sacks.

I stopped at the Farmers Elevator in Bellingham in 2017, and the old elevator building was still there, intact with the milling operation. I talked to the guy in that place, and he explained that milling was part of his routine job when a customer came to have that done.

To operate, the mill had electric starters to get both mill heads spinning at a standard speed. Next, the mill was adjusted for fine, medium, or coarse, and then the grain started to flow into the mill. My dad had a device on the open top grain chute that fed grain to the mill. It was a strong electromagnet where a thin layer of grain flowed into the mill, and it would catch any nails or tools left in the grain by mistake. Obviously, if that happened, it could cost thousands of dollars in repairs and shut down the mill for days or weeks. (And a disaster like that was very dangerous.)

Of the various elevators in our area, as far as I knew, the Farmers Elevator in Bellingham was the only one that did state-of-the-art milling (as of the 1920s). The only other mill, in Madison 10 miles away, had old turn-of-the-century equipment. Bellingham was a "full service" operation, with the ability to grind many different ways.

The main maintenance required on the mill was to replace the removable grinding plates, maybe every 6 to 12 months. To prolong their life, the mill rotation could be reversed periodically. The replacement was a 5- to 15-hour job by two experienced people, my dad John and Ed Frosch. Just removing and replacing 16 grinding plates (8 plates each on 2 mill wheels) was a mechanic's job—unbolt the old, bolt on the new. The main job was rebalancing each spinning mill head. Imagine tons of rotating mass, spinning very rapidly—even a wee bit unbalanced—and the whole thing would vibrate itself to destruction. (Consider balancing car wheels and tires.)

I am sure the manufacture of each mill surface was required to come from the factory under rigid specifications. In addition to being balanced, all together, the combined grinding surface (8 surfaces against 8 surfaces) each had to be perfectly flat, and the one flat totally parallel related to the other flat, all rotating and not vibrating at "umpteen" revolutions per minute—the whole rotating process being maybe 1 or 2 tons. So I considered when my dad and Ed Frosch got everything operating right, it was time for a beer.

In later years, as an optical (spectroscopy) chemist, I could appreciate how well they did the mill repair job, after working with or setting up optically flat equipment so the photons of light would go where I expected them to go.

When I helped my dad in the elevator between 1940 and 1945, I usually did the milling or else occasionally the whole shebang, when he needed to be away a few hours if a customer or relative died, and he needed to go to the funeral.

❧ *Chapter 21* ❧

John the Butcher

Growing up on the farm, and being the second son of the family, I am sure that John, from when he was little on, helped with the family butchering. However, I never heard any stories about that from my dad or other family members like John's dad, Grandpa Peter, or his brothers or sisters, particularly his brother Wilbert.

The exception to this was my dad's story about being assigned the job of building a smokehouse in the timeframe of about 1914-1920. Of course, the smokehouse was for smoking fresh-made meat products to add to their flavor and increase acceptance by the family. In later years, my dad explained he was left on his own, but secured information from relatives and books on how to build the smokehouse to be most efficient, how long to smoke specific meats and what wood to use to give what flavors. Over the years growing up, I tasted these meats and remember that they were good, particularly sausages and blood sausages.

What I learned about butchering I got by helping my dad and Wilbert actually butcher animals. They operated together as a team, each knowing his part, and not even explaining what was going on. When I was too little, I just watched. Later, I was told to do things for the group activity.

Actually, this is a good way to teach something, and to get it right. One reads about this way of teaching by having an apprentice, as in stories about Ben Franklin, where, if a kid wanted to be a printer, he started in as an apprentice.

In my time, I had a son named Eric who wanted to be a meteorologist. During his junior and senior years of high school, we visited a number of colleges, and he chose to go to Penn State. After studying it and reviewing it, I told him I did not think the family could afford for him to go there. He/we settled on his going to University of Maryland, College Park, since that meant in-state tuition and he could use a small scholarship to help pay his way. I did agree that, if he did that, I would help some in the cost for his Master's degree. That turned out to be a good decision, since in his last 2 years at University of Maryland, Eric worked at Goddard for the Meteorology Department part time. He was essentially working as an intern or apprentice, as in Ben Franklin's times, starting by doing many menial computer chores, and being a go-fer for the researchers. By the time he finished his Bachelor's degree, he had a good background with the meteorologists at Goddard, and by then knew what he wanted to do in graduate school, so he was in demand to get a good post in several graduate schools.

When I was about 9 or 11 years old, I began to help my dad and Uncle Wilbert with pig butchering. First, the pig was selected from the herd. It was taken out in the barnyard and held on the ground. Then Wilbert would take his well-calibrated hammer and knock the pig on the head, being careful to only knock it out, not to kill it. Next, Ray accumulated about one-half a bucket of clean snow. Wilbert stuck the pig with his long, curved, razor-sharp knife and cut the jugular vein in the neck. I would be holding the edge of the bucket tightly against the pig's throat and would catch the spurting blood (from an artery) in the bucket, furiously stirring it into the snow to quickly cool it. This was to prevent clotting, which would have made it worthless for blood sausage. We had two goals: to collect the blood and to remove all the blood to give a better-quality meat.

Once when we did this, about the time no more blood was flowing, the pig returned to consciousness, broke loose from our holding it, and took several steps before it collapsed and died. I saw how a mammal dies from loss of blood.

Let me digress with a story; yes, it is still about John. I was delivering papers on the south side of Bellingham (at about 12 or 13) when I heard a screech of tires on pavement, a crash, and an abrupt screech of brakes as a local train stopped. I rushed to the site (two blocks) and saw that a vehicle had been hit by the train as he tried to cross the railroad tracks in front of the train. A lot of people gathered in minutes. The bottom line: The driver had his left arm out the window as he was hit by the train, and the arm was mangled. A guy with a pickup was there, and my dad had me get a mattress from our house. It was placed on the truck bed, the injured guy was placed on it by the surrounding people, including the town doctor, and the blood was squirting out of the injured arm. And then, surprise, the doctor got in the truck's seat, not in the back to stop the artery spurting blood. My first thought was The guy is surely a goner, and he was.

Back to butchering: After the pig collapsed and died, Wilbert had the job to shave (cut) the hair of the outside of the carcass. The reason is that on some cuts of pork, the hide is left on. Next, a cut was made down the middle of the belly of the pig, and all that stuff inside, such as intestines, heart, stomach, and liver, was removed by John and Wilbert. I didn't help.

Then the inside was cleaned out. The pig was cut into halves, then quarters, then into routine cuts of pork. I was brought into the job again with the processing and preparing of the meat.

Just as with hunters and gatherers of ancient times, my dad (and his family) knew how to use almost all of the pig. For example, for a number of years we made sausage tubes from cleaned small intestines. However, they did not use the pig bristles from the hide; it was cheaper to buy pig bristle paint brushes until, in later years, brushes were made of synthetic fibers.

After my dad cut up the pig into typical types of pork such as hams, shoulder roasts, and pork chops, he then trimmed these to separate fat and lean. Included in the lean meat was a certain amount of less desirable lean meat, all for sausage, blood sausage, and hamburger. My dad's recipe for good hamburger was ground beef plus about 15 to 20 percent lean pork. My job was to take the pork for sausage and grind it in a hand-crank grinder. For regular sausage, this was thoroughly mixed, and seasoning was added by mixing to taste. My dad was the mixer and seasoner-to-taste. I worried, seeing him tasting mixed raw pork. Eating raw pork could cause trichinosis, then as now. I guess he tasted a bit, then spit it out.

Blood sausage was made separately. The ground pork used for it at our house was mixed in a cleaned, galvanized washtub. The pig's blood was mixed with the ground meat.

Then each sausage ring was pressed into a casing with a sausage press. This press had about a 3-gallon capacity, with a plate the size of the inside of the press bucket, forced down by a screen run by a rotating handle. I ran the press, and my dad put casings on the press outlet nozzle, then guided the formation of rings of sausage. The sausage was cooked by my mother and then frozen until thawed, cooked more, and eaten. Some of it was instead canned for longer storage before eating. Also, a significant part of cooked sausage was packed into cheap, grey cylindrical crockery jars that were typically 3 feet high and 18 inches in diameter. After packing them in tightly, the sausage was covered with molten hot lard to preserve it for long periods. I remember my mom sent me down to the cellar as a little kid to get a ring of sausage that we were to have for Sunday breakfast. Cooked bacon was also preserved in the same way, in tall crocks in molten/congealed lard.

Another activity of butchering was Mom cutting as much fat as possible off the pork, then rendering (melting) it into lard and cracklings. Besides using much lard for long-term storage of sausage and bacon, it was also used in all kinds of cooking for bread, cookies, and fried potatoes. One of my favorite uses was cooking doughnuts in molten lard. Another was that once in a while Mom made fried bread dough. She pulled it out fairly flat, fried it on both sides, and then sprinkled it with sugar while hot, before serving. The cracklings left from rendering lard were saved and added to cornbread, a tasty treat, particularly when covered with strawberry rhubarb jelly.

We usually butchered in mid-October, hopefully after a snowfall. There was no refrigeration then (1930-1940) so my dad had a sea-trunk, left over from its use as a trunk for the back of our 1928 Pontiac on vacation trips. (Later, cars came with built-in "trunks" in the back end.) My dad would put the trunk on the north side of the house, bank snow around it, and splash water on the snow to form ice. This would be our freezer for uncooked meats from butchering until thaws usually in early April. In later years, we got an icebox, then a freezer locker at the town butcher shop, and still later a refrigerator and freezer.

Besides pigs, most of the time we had two milk cows, and if the calves were male, they usually got butchered as veal, or baby beef. Female calves could be sold to dairy farmers (most farmers were), since they had to bring in new breeding stock, or otherwise they had problems with inbreeding in a closed herd. Of course, we had chickens; my mom had us raise chickens as a cash crop to supplement my dad's salary. One can't just be a layabout in a growing family and expect the family income to be enough. Typically, about Saturday noon when I was 8 or 10 years old and later, my mom would send me out to pick out the oldest cock, chop off its head, scald it, and pick off the feathers (including pin feathers) and bring it to her to cook as Sunday dinner. My memory is that those days she cooked it in the pressure cooker; that was quick, and the meat was tender and tasty. I never did think to see if the bones were edible like in canned salmon, which is steam-pressure cooked.

My dad would usually take off a half-day on a Saturday to do this butchering. The rest of the meat processing was done in the evenings after work.

Another source of meat for our family was pheasants. (See Hunting, in an earlier chapter.) My job after getting pheasants was to remove the bottom end of the legs, the feet, and skin the bird. I gave it to Mom in that form. It took about 1 to 3 minutes per bird. My mother then filleted it, cutting the meat off the body and detaching the drumsticks and wings. Pheasant is good eating, at least the way Mom made it. We ate pheasant burgers, canned pheasant, roasted pheasant, baked pheasant, and pheasant and dumplings (not like Eastern Shore dumplings but the kind of raised dumpling one drops onto the pheasant gravy as the last step, just before the pheasant is done). I once was taken to dinner by a company as part of a meeting where they were courting us to buy one of their chemical lubricants for yarn manufacturing. We ate in the board of directors' private dining room. Pheasant under glass was prepared by the company chef. It was all right, but not at all close to my mother's recipes.

In the butchering saga, we once had a bull calf that got to be a yearling before we got around to butchering it. For all cuts of beef, this was the best I ever ate. I think that now there is a niche market in yearling beef for those who can afford it. Of course, it would not be for dedicated beef-eaters, who seem to think beef has to be tough and stringy. That's my perception, anyway.

Finally in the butchering saga, my dad John also made hams. They were preserved by injecting them with a brine-salt solution in which various spices were added according to my dad's recipe. After that, the ham was dried, fitted with a piece of twine around the bone, and dipped into molten wax (like that used to seal a fruit jar of jelly or jam) and cooled. This formed a wax layer on the outside of the ham. This was hung from a nail in the rafter in the cool cellar. As usual, my mom would send me down to the cellar to get a ham for Sunday dinner. She spent a lot of time soaking the ham in hot water to remove excess salt, and then cooked it. I had a friend who told me years later that until he was 22 years old, he believed that the best part of the ham was the white meat—in other words, the fat. And then someone explained that you weren't supposed to eat that part! I am not much for ham, but my wife,

Barbie, made great hambone kidney bean soup. In getting it ready, she split the bone to expose the marrow inside the bone to add more taste and nourishment to the soup.

❖ Chapter 22 ❖

Family Crises

Around about 1928, my brother Gerard developed a childhood disease that there was no cure for in those days. He died at age 6, shortly before he was supposed to start school like his brothers. As his sickness progressed, it was obvious that he would die. Near the end, he had made his First Communion, and Gerard told Dad, "Daddy, don't be sad, since tomorrow I will be in heaven with Jesus. And besides, I don't think I want to go to school after all."

———◦◦◇◦◦———

Around the same time, my 4-year-old brother Don also was subject to a disease that damaged his ears and his hearing. That was controlled for several years, but it flared up again 4 or 5 years later, after we had moved to Minnesota. Locally the doctors did not know what to do, so they recommended a surgeon in Minneapolis to operate on it to save his life. Minneapolis was about 200 miles away, so my dad took off from work, and Mom and Dad took him for the operation.

They were gone about 10 days and came back with Don in better shape. Ear problems continued through school (through college) and until his death at 62. I do not know how much this operation cost, but Dad made an agreement to pay a certain amount each month—that was the system in those days; they call that personal responsibility.

Eventually, over many years, my dad got the debt paid off. Of course, it was quite a drain on the family finances; my dad did not complain.

———∞◇∞———

We were visiting the Ben Kelzer family, and a group of Hackert and Kelzer kids was playing dog sledding with the Kelzer family dog. At some point, the dog objected to pulling the wagon (sled) and turned back on the rider, Don, and bit his leg.

Don was taken to the doctor and ended up on crutches for a while. He had to go through a series of rabies shots, but he remained healthy.

Chapter 23

Family Finances

As a little kid, I knew about family financial problems but was too young to help deal with them. But by 1942, when I was 14, I was involved. About October, we visited the Ray Baker family in Milbank, South Dakota, on a Saturday evening, and Dad and I looked at a new Chevrolet, which seemed something the family could handle. Our '37 Ford had bald tires and many miles on it. Dad seemed interested but wavered on buying it, and did not. Within about a month, World War II started, and a new car was verboten.

Dad was very good with finances in his business at the elevator. This included keeping elaborate books as required by a co-op operation. As I grew older, I became aware of his accounting procedures, including those for audits.

As I said elsewhere, Dad had a running awareness or knowledge of what the dollar status of the elevator was every day; he knew what he paid for the grain coming in, and he sold it favorably day by day. This is the business philosophy of elevator managers even today. (As described earlier, I have gone around the country and asked them what happened to them when corn's price had recently dropped abruptly, and they said it didn't really matter, because they kept their buying and selling of the grain each day approximately equal.)

When Dad left the grain business in 1945, he could have gotten a job in finance or banking, but that wasn't his primary interest.

The family, of course, had our occasional financial problems. An example was when a cow abruptly died, and buying a replacement meant about a $100 outlay. I think some of my savings went into that since I had some income and saved regularly.

A later example was that we had a family conference when the dairy operation came up for sale, and this meant a lot of work for all; of course we bought it and it was successful.

I wrote about another example in the section "Family Crises," when the family had large medical bills to pay off.

My dad's training of me in my youth helped me understand business in general. Later in life, when I worked at DuPont, there was a fifth of a million dollars' worth of ingredients that had gone bad due to a weather situation. I was able to suggest to the accountants a common-sense way to deal with it—I proposed they put the loss into a suspense account, and then over the months distribute the loss into the plant's other business expenses.

In later years at the store in St. Cloud, Dad eventually got his son Don (an accountant) to keep the books and do the taxes. Even as Dad's life was waning, I visited one time and he was upset because he and Mom were eating into their savings; he calculated that he would be broke in, say, 3 years and would have to go on the dole. I told him not to pinch pennies. He had six kids, all doing well—so not to worry. When he died, each got a small inheritance.

What I have to say here is speculation, since I never have heard any details about Grandpa Peter's finances, except the obvious, such as that son John was given a farm when he married. As I have said elsewhere, the Peter Hackert homestead was run essentially as a subsistence operation. They grew most of all they used in the way of food, made stuff that other people bought, like soap and ropes, had an icehouse and made and stored ice. Grandpa Peter even grew his own pipe tobacco, even though in Minnesota people said it could not be done. Their cash crop was wheat.

The part of the story I never heard was that in World War I, wheat was selling for $5 a bushel, and if Grandpa could get, say, 3000 bushels over several years, that would add up to $15,000. In those days, one could build a multi-bedroom two-story house for maybe $2500. Grandpa

Peter, with John's help and others, built the house that was on the farm about 1918. This included a building for doing the laundry, and also a smokehouse—built by John. This is reasonable, since in 1945, we moved to St. Cloud and Dad bought a big old house near his grocery store for $3500.

I have read at least five economics books and am aware that in the 1920s, the bank in Bellingham went bankrupt, and Uncle Frank, who worked there, was out of a job. Apparently, if Grandpa Peter had his money stashed in that bank, he got it out before the crash. It was a crash, since by the middle 1920s, the bankers in New York, Chicago, Minneapolis, St. Louis, and Denver realized that the Midwest farmers collectively had more money than they had, and could possibly buy them out. So the big city bankers got the Federal Reserve and government to issue rules that drove many Midwest small banks into bankruptcy, according to these economics books.

Thank God Grandpa Peter was astute enough to avoid going broke in this catastrophe. My understanding is that Grandpa Peter paid for a college education for Frank, John's older brother. Lucy, John's younger sister, got her education and joined the Benedictine Sisters at St. Joe, Minnesota. (She was named Sister Venard; Lucy was her name from birth.) Grandpa Peter's sister was Sister Freda at the Benedictine convent in St. Joe.

Often, when I was a kid growing up, when we went to St. Cloud to see Mom's relatives, we would go visit Sisters Venard and Freda. When I got to be of college age, I guess, I was expected to go to St. John's University, the Benedictine monastery and university at Collegeville, Minnesota, several miles from St. Joe. Of course, Uncle Frank did his college stuff there, and my brother Don was at St. John's as a sophomore, when we moved from Bellingham to St. Cloud in 1945.

Back to Grandpa Peter's giving farms (or a college education) to his kids: As mentioned previously, John was supposed to get the homeplace and farm it. But my dad John was not to be a farmer, so Wilbert got the farm, and Alvin got the South Forty (acres). I do not know about how Peter's daughters Mary and Elizabeth made out. They married and lived on farms next to each other near Rosen. Mary (Spors) lived across the road from Uncle John Stolpmann on a farm.

Eventually, Grandpa Peter moved to Nassau, Minnesota, and lived across the street from brother-in-law Frank Kanthak and Peter's sister. I remember this very well since Edwin Kanthak, Frank's son, farmed between Nassau and Bellingham, and I helped him one summer when I was 15 or 16, but he lived in Nassau at his parents' house. So in the evening, we would go to his home and I could go across the street to see Grandpa Peter (and enjoy Grandma Ida's cookies).

One evening, when I was going home to Nassau with Edwin, there was an adventure. As Ed started up the pickup truck, he noticed the gas gauge was pointing to empty; he was supposed to have gassed up when we left in the morning. He figured we would probably have to walk part way when the truck stalled, so after he got the engine quite hot, with him working the gas pedal, I poured 1 to 2 gallons of diesel fuel he had for the tractor into the gas tank. It smoked profusely, and he had to work the gas pedal to keep going. We drove the 8 miles to Nassau, shifting back and forth from third to second gear to keep the engine turning fast and hot. At Nassau, we stopped at the gas station with the engine running erratically. (We probably would not have gotten the engine started again if it stopped on the diesel fuel.) As the gasoline poured into the tank, the engine ran smoother and smoother, and with a full tank of gas plus a little diesel, the engine idled normally. In retrospect, if Edwin was having problems with sticking valves, that problem was fixed for at least 6 months.

Another adventure we had out harvesting at Edwin's was this: When planting the wheat field, it had been quite dry, but then when cutting the wheat with the binder (cutting it into bundles to thresh it after drying it in shocks) it had been rainy, so at least an acre or more around the water hole (slough) was too damp to run the tractor there. We got the team of horses hitched to a hayrack and tied a chain from the back of the wagon to the tractor. I drove the horses and wagon, pulling the tractor through the moist ground while cutting the wheat into bundles. Farmers have to be innovative to get as much as possible harvested. (That means dollars in their pockets.)

❧ Chapter 24 ❧

John and Cars

As I mentioned before, from my earliest memories in North Dakota, after my dad finished work and supper was over, occasionally we all would pile into the car and drive around the country. Especially in spring when the wild flowers were in bloom, we witnessed the grand fragrance of all kinds of plants and new mown hay.

In those days, he had a 1928 Pontiac Sedan. I was a traveler, even then, so I was always ready to go with Dad to the store, or to get something fixed on the car. I wrote earlier about the time when, coming home with me standing in front of the right front seat, Dad slammed on the brakes and my head bumped into the windshield and broke it. My dad said that he should have warned me. Dad bought a new windshield and installed it with my help. I held the tools for him.

Later, when we had moved to Bellingham and I was 6 or 7, Dad made a deal with his cousin Joe. Joe had this Model T Ford but the engine had stopped working. The car was brought to our place and Dad worked on it in his spare time; while it was being fixed, the car was outside the elevator. The deal was that my dad John was to get it in shape, and Joe would give him a half a hog. In those days, there was a lot of bartering going on (and still is). I watched (and helped a little) while Dad took the engine apart, ground the valves and valve seats, made sure the pistons were OK and used a new one where necessary, installed new piston rings and crankshaft bearings, and repaired other things like the carburetor and oil and gas line pumps. Finally, all was reassembled, and it ran.

This all took several months working outside. The unassembled car and parts were covered over with an old piece of plasticized tablecloth to keep out dirt and rain. (This was during the drought years, so it probably never got rained on.) And late in the fall at butchering time, Joe brought us half a hog; we had pigs but with an extra earned one, the hog of ours was then eventually sent to South St. Paul where we got money for it.

By the time I was about 12, we had traded our Pontiac for a 1937 Ford. My dad taught me how to clean and gap the spark plugs, install a new ignition point set, adjust the ignition timing, replace tires and tubes, rotate the wheels, and change the oil. So slowly, I became the family mechanic, taking a load off my dad, who was always very busy.

In the early fall, I would winterize the car. For instance, I would put fresh oil in the car; it is awkward to do that with the car in a snowbank in the winter. In non-snowy times, to change the oil, I would park the car over a depression in the yard so I could get underneath. (We had sheds on the property, but couldn't use them for cars because most of the time they were occupied by pigs and calves and grain storage.) I would also gap the plugs somewhat wider, which was supposed to give easier starting in very cold weather.

The one thing my dad got for the car that everyone appreciated was a built-in gasoline heater. It would put out quite hot air almost immediately, as opposed to the Pontiac that had an engine manifold heater that slowly gave off lukewarm heat. In traveling in the Pontiac, all except the front seat passengers had to have blankets, along with heavy winter coats, caps, and gloves. This 1937 Ford was better than the Pontiac in that it almost always started and went, particularly in winter.

In those days, sometimes we kids traveled in Grandpa Peter's old car. He had a horse blanket we could cover ourselves with. It was the hide of a horse, thoroughly processed so it was very soft and warm.

I suppose that kind of horse blanket was used when riding around in an open horse-drawn wagon in early times. For example, when John was about 4 years old, Grandpa Peter took him along (in an open wagon) to bring wheat to Madison about 15 miles away. They were to grind it into flour for the Hackert kitchen to make bread and cakes. This trip took all day out in the winter cold, so having a heavy blanket was critical.

Another step in winterizing the car was to add an extra layer of glass to the flat windshield with an air layer between the two glasses to keep frost from blinding the view out. In addition, we had an electric fan with rubber open blades to blow hot air from the gasoline heater onto the windshield.

When I was 17, I had earned enough money to buy myself a car similar to my dad's. So I had the two cars to care for along with all the other chores. My dad's Ford ran for years with trips to the grandparents in St. Cloud, to North Dakota, and to New York City in 1939. It was used for hauling for the cattle and pigs and chickens, and after 1945, for delivering groceries for a number of years. As I've said before, in these later years, my dad stopped changing the oil since it leaked or burned away. What Dad did was to make a deal with the garage/gas station people across the street from the store. They saved some of the not-so-dirty oil from oil changes and Dad paid them 5 cents a quart; he just kept adding this used oil as needed. (Save a buck – make a buck.)

And don't forget the story of when Dad, Don and I fixed Don's car, and we got two sets of parts from Sears by accident when we had only ordered one.

In the grocery store, as in Bellingham, the '37 Ford was used for business. I was staying at home and going to St. John's University (for chemistry), so I helped Dad on evenings or weekends. He would be buying one-half of a steer at the wholesale meat company, so I would go with the car to pick it up and bring it to him for his meat market operation. I would also do maintenance on the car that was needed for the business.

When I was about 15, as I said before, my dad and I would go pheasant hunting on a Sunday afternoon. We would be in an empty field where grain like wheat had been grown, and only the stubble was left. Dad suggested I try driving, which I did. There was no lane to follow and no obstructions, so I could get the feel of steering and braking. Soon I was assigned off-the-road jobs like hooking up a trailer and driving from our barnyard to the adjacent field to get several loads of straw from a neighbor's straw stack (made by threshing wheat) for the pigs and cows. At times, we had two cows so we could have continuous milk supply. Later, driving became more commercial, like hauling hay for the dairy herd. Driving, of course, went along with looking after the car. At 15, I got my driver's license at the Rosen store. This involved filling out a form and paying 50 cents.

Besides the car, Dad also got me exposed to handling horses. In the time of our dairy operation, I would borrow a team of horses for specific jobs like getting rid of the winter manure pile by spreading it with a manure spreader on the field adjacent to our property. The owner of the field got the manure for fertilizer and supplied the spreader and horses. The farmer's place was about 6 miles north of town, so borrowing the team and equipment involved lengthy trips back and forth. When I was a kid, the farmer would come at my dad's request to plow our two gardens for spring planting. We would keep the team overnight for several days if we needed it, so my job was to feed and water them. By the time I was 15, I signed on to this farmer's threshing crew, so I knew their horses, their handling, etc. Brother Don and I ran a bundle wagon, delivering bundles of cut grain to the threshing machine, acting together as "one man" of about ten in the threshing crew since we were only teenagers. Of course, at dinner break we ate as two men!

❧ *Chapter 25* ❧

John and Houses

The house in this photo from Geraldine Koshiol is most probably the house on the Grandpa Peter farm that was on the property when he homesteaded it in 1897 as a 27-year-old. Apparently, a better house was built sometime after that. When I was 5 years old, and we had arrived in Minnesota from North Dakota (1932), there was the "new" house my dad had helped build on the Grandpa Peter farm around 1916. In addition, there was an old house that had been moved (my speculation) from where the "new" house then stood, to a place near the entrance to the driveway. (On entering the driveway, this old house was on one's left.)

In later years, a drive-through corncrib stood there. My understanding was, probably from my dad, that Grandpa Peter used the old house for his tools and woodworking. The corn crib was built, as was normal then, with two cribs side by side, with space to drive between and a roof over all of it.

In later years, Wilbert fixed cars in that drive-through space. At one time, a car fell off the jack, and Wilbert was trapped underneath. They found him at suppertime when they realized he was not around and got him out alive (just able to breathe a little).

Grandpa Peter Sr., who lived on what was later known to me as the Conrad Hackert farm, made violins, and also did coffins on request. Probably according to my dad, one of the violins that Grandpa Peter Sr. made was owned and used for years. If you could look at Conrad Hackert's tombstone, you'd see he was well known for many things, including being a fiddler. In his day, a significant recreation was public dances. (Note the story of Dad's dad, Grandpa Peter getting the Halloween Dance prize for the best costume, dressed as an old lady and dancing all evening with the young bucks and other men, who were later quite embarrassed.)

In later years, my cousins told me that Great Grandpa Peter Sr., first lived on that farm, and his son Conrad had it when I was a kid and growing up in Minnesota. See "Chapter 2 – The Hackerts Arrive in America."

When my dad John married and went to work as the elevator manager in Bellingham (1921), he and Mom lived in the first or second house north of the Norwegian Lutheran church along Highway 75, down the hill from the water tower. During those years, Ralph and Gerard were born. When they moved to Anamoose, North Dakota, in 1924, they rented a house on the edge of town close to the elevator. The house was on the end of a street across the railroad tracks from the elevator. The property had a barn where Dad kept a cow for fresh milk for the growing family of kids; Don (Donald), Ray (Raymond), Katie (Kathryn), and

Gerry (Geraldine) were born there. The property was big enough for a large garden, fenced-in chickens, and a lot of room for us kids to play, like croquet, marbles, and driving our play car and tricycles. The barn was most likely used for horses for family transportation up until a few years before cars.

When we moved again to Bellingham in 1932, we first lived in a house with a barn for our milk cow and a small garden. This house was the second house north of the Presbyterian church. We only lived there for several months, but Rusty (Lucille) was born there. A couple months later, we moved to a 5-acre lot across the road from the elevator (to the south of it) with a house, barn, sheds, and chicken house, along with one big garden. We developed another toward the back of the property, which was part of a hay field. Then we expanded the property by renting the adjacent 30 acres as pasture space for our dairy herd. The family lived at this place for 13 years.

When my dad and mom moved to St. Cloud, they lived at the corner of 10th Street and 3rd Avenue South for many years in a big old house (two full stories, and a full basement with sleeping and kitchen facilities, along with utilities such as a furnace).

About the time of Dad's retirement, the old house was condemned to make way for St. Cloud College facilities, so Dad and Mom bought and lived in north St. Cloud. Later in retirement, they lived at the Benedict Center on the edge of east St. Cloud and remained there until they died.

✦ *Chapter 26* ✦

More Memories

Six Grandmas

When I was about 20, it occurred to me when growing up that I may have had maybe six grandmas. I brought this idea up with Alfred Volkenant, a cousin of my dad John. I explained to him that during my youth, we would go to Frank Kanthak's, and there would be a grandma with a grey shawl around her shoulders rocking in her chair in the living room, knitting vigorously. We would go see the Volkenants (again my dad's cousin's family), and there would be a grandma knitting in the parlor. And so it went, going to another three or four cousins' homes.

Alfred told me it was the same grandma, the stepmother of Grandpa Peter. She would stay with one daughter for a while until she and the family decided that was enough. The son-in-law would load all the grandma's possessions into the pickup truck, including her rocking chair, and take her to another daughter's house.

———◦◦◦◦◦◦◦———

A story about my sister Katie was that in the period of late 1930s to 1945, my dad and mom recognized that Katie was somewhat of a problem child. So at supper, she sat between Mom and Dad. Mom was left-handed and Dad was right-handed, so Katie sat to the left of Mom and right of Dad. When something happened, for example some kid spilled his or her milk, Katie got it from both sides even if she had done nothing.

In later years, when Katie was about 25 years old, she told me that she got punished for a lot of things she did not do, but also got away with other things, and probably ended up with a positive balance.

Actually, Katie was a very independent thinker and had a lot of interesting observations of life. She was usually the leader of the table talk, much of it humorous. In comparison, Dad always got the St. Paul daily paper and the Catholic newspaper *The Wanderer* (in German). Many times, the conversation was about USA and world news (like World War II) and news related to the Catholic Church. (Obviously, Dad translated the news from German to English for family consumption.)

About 1933, I was visiting Grandpa Peter's and "helped" Wilbert and Peter make ice to store in their icehouse. There was plenty of sawdust around from personal woodworking and from friends and relatives, with many knowing carpentry and woodcraft. Sawdust was used to store the ice and keep it cold. When they brought in a bucket of ice, there was a fish frozen in it. After they cut the block smaller with the fish still in the ice, they gave it to me. We put it in a bucket of cold water and it melted, and then the fish started swimming around! That was really something for a kid who was 5 years old! Jesus rising from the dead! That's the sort of thing a little kid thinks! (It was not dead of course; it was a cold-blooded fish.)

We could breed our pigs at our place, and then we'd have little piglets. By the time they were about 10 days to 2 weeks old, the males would have to be castrated, or later the meat would be rank. Females were fine. Male pheasants were as good as females. We'd also eat the male prairie chickens and chickens...no problem with the meat.

When we lived in Bellingham, I slept on the open porch upstairs. One morning there was a great commotion outside at dawn. Apparently, a stray dog had come into our yard and was chasing chickens and making a loud noise, barking and so forth. By the time I got out of bed, I saw my dad coming out of the house with his shotgun. He decided not to shoot the dog but to shoot down into the gravel by the house, which kind of bounced and skinned the dog on one side. The dog abruptly ran off, howling continuously and racing rapidly out of sight and sound. My dad told me afterward he was concerned that if he shot the dog, if there was an owner, he would come and give Dad a hard time about abusing his favorite dog. So he said that, if the dog came home bruised and the owner complained about it to Dad, he would charge the owner $15 for each of the chickens the dog killed.

My dad kept his car next to the driveway into the elevator. One day I happened to be looking that way from our house across the road and Dad came out of the elevator to come home for lunch. He got into the car, started to back up, bumped it into a power line pole, and knocked the pole over. I went over and he said, smiling, that pole must have walked over behind the car when he was not looking. And he said that it probably was a pretty rotten pole anyway, from the look of it, since such a small bump knocked it over!

One spring Sunday, we were at Mass—probably on First Communion Sunday. Early in the Mass, I looked up and Dad had jumped over three or five pews ahead of us—thump, thump, thump—to a little girl, probably a second-grader, who was part of a group of girls dressed in white with crepe paper ribbon in their hair and carrying candles. One had set the hair ribbon next to her on fire. In a matter of several seconds, my dad got to her and beat the fire out with his bare hands. Of course, the nun in charge had all the candles put out. I thought that my dad John was pretty spry for an old guy—of about 33!

In Conclusion…

I hope I have entertained and taught you with these stories of my dad's life. I tried to do as Jesus did, when he taught through stories. But just as the Bible only contains a fraction of all that happened in Jesus's life, I included many of my memories and those shared by family and others, but not everything.

Sincerely,
Ray

PART 3

*Pictures of People, Places, and Things
Mentioned in "My Dad John"*

Peter Hackert Sr., around 1890

Mathilda Stolpmann Hackert
Second wife of Peter Hackert Sr., around 1890

Mathilda Stolpmann Hackert was the grandma in the "Six Grandmas" story. She was born April 17, 1848 in Germany, where she married Peter Hackert in 1875, and died February 4, 1935 in the Rosen area.

Sons of Peter Hackert, Sr.

Front: Edwin and Conrad, sons of Mathilda Stolpmann

Back: John (who owned the John Hackert Building in Nassau), Albert, Grandpa Peter, sons of Susanna Roggenbuck.

Alexander (son of Peter and Mathilda) was born and died in 1888.

Daughters of Peter Hackert, Sr. and Mathilda Stolpmann, around 1895

Agnes, Rosalia, and Appolonia

Peter Sr. had two other daughters, Suzanna with Susanna Roggenbuck, and Rinata with Mathilda Stolpmann, who each died before their first birthdays

Grandpa Peter Herman Hackert and his first wife, Martha Semrau Hackert, parents of my dad John, around July 1893.

They were married July 1, 1893; this may be their wedding picture.

Grandpa Peter and his five children from Martha Semrau Hackert
1908 - probably shortly after her death

Front: Grandpa Peter, Elizabeth, Lucy

Back: Frank, Mary, my dad John

Grandpa Peter and second wife, Ida Romana Voigt Hackert, 1910

They wed January 25, 1910; this was probably their wedding picture.

Grandpa Peter and Ida Voigt Hackert, 1940

Photographed for their 30th wedding anniversary

The family of Grandpa Peter and Ida, 1940
Grandma Ida and Grandpa Peter's 30th wedding anniversary

Front: Elizabeth, Bernice, Ida, Grandpa Peter, Alvin (known as Pete, twin to Alice)

Back: Mary, my dad John, Lucy (Sister Venard), Frank, Alice, Wilbert

Ignatius "Shorty" Voigt, around 1915

Ignatius was a poet. When our family would get together, he'd go out in a field or out on the porch and write a poem.

Ignatius and Mary Kraemer Schreder Voigt
with her children, around 1920

Front: Grandma Mary, Alma (Sister Edwardelle), Hildy, Grandpa Ignatius (Mary's second husband), Roman (Father Steven)

Back: William (Father William), Anna, Matt, Ed, Peter, my mother Marie (born Mary), Leo (order uncertain)

Ignatius Voigt and six Schreder boys, around 1920

The male children of Grandma Mary and Steven Schreder (Mary's first husband)

Roman (Father Steven), Matt, Leo, William (Father William), Peter, Ed, Ignatius Voigt (order uncertain)

Grandpa Ignatius Voigt dragging a field, May 1944

In those days, a drag harrow was used to loosen and even out soil after it had been plowed and packed. This was similar to raking a garden.

Grandpa Ignatius Voigt and Grandma Mary Kraemer Schreder Voigt, 1951

Photographed for their 35th wedding anniversary

Grandpa Ignatius and Grandma Mary Voigt and family, June 1959

Front: Hildy (Hildegard), Sister Edwardelle (Alma), Grandpa Ignatius, Grandma Mary

Back: Peter, Anna, Leo, Father William, Father Steven (Roman), Marie

Photographed during a celebration for Father William when he became a Third Order Regular Franciscan

Young John (my dad)

Marie and John's wedding, June 21, 1921

Marie and John, newlyweds, 1921

Marie's visit to Grandpa Ignatius' Montana horse ranch, around 1925

Dad and Mom

Sons of Marie and John in the yard in Anamoose, North Dakota,
around 1927

Ralph, Ray (Raymond), Gerard, Don (Donald)

The Hackert boys, summer of 1927

Gerard, age 3

Don, age 2   Ralph, age 5,

Ray, born March 1927

Marie and sons, around 1928

Playing croquet north of home in Anamoose, North Dakota

Marie, Ray, Gerard, Ralph, Don (order uncertain)

John and Marie's Family, around 1935

Front: Ralph, Katie (Kathryn), Gerry (Geraldine), Ray (Raymond)

Back: John, Marie, Rusty (Lucille), Marie's sister Hildy (Hildegard), Don (Donald)

On the trip to the 1939 New York World's Fair

Ray, Don, our cousin Jerry

Near Uncle Frank's house, where we stayed while
visiting the World's Fair

At the 1939 World's Fair in Queens, NY

Front: Ray, my cousin Jerry

Back: Dad, Mom, Don

Katie came to the World's Fair but was not with us in this picture. Ralph was old enough that he stayed home to work at the elevator. Gerry and Rusty were too little to come, and stayed with Uncle Wilbert.

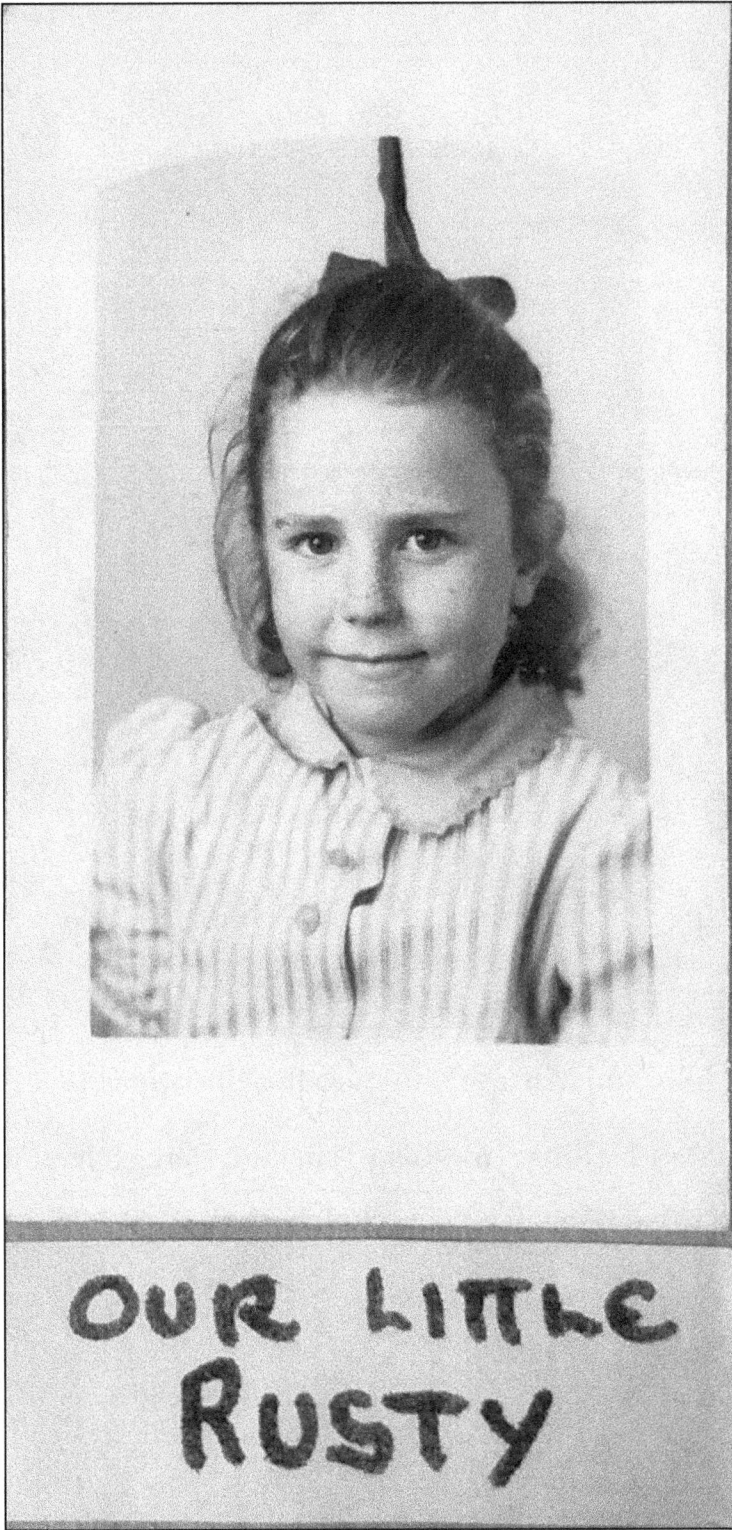

Rusty (Lucille), around 1940

John and Marie's family, around Christmas 1940

Front: Katie (Kathryn), Rusty (Lucille), Gerry (Geraldine)

Back: Don (Donald), Mom, Ralph, Dad, Ray (Raymond)

Ralph at Pasadena, California,

Army Engineering School, August 1943

Mom, Ralph, and Dad, October 24, 1943

Ralph on leave from the Army

Don, Mom, and Dad, October 24, 1943

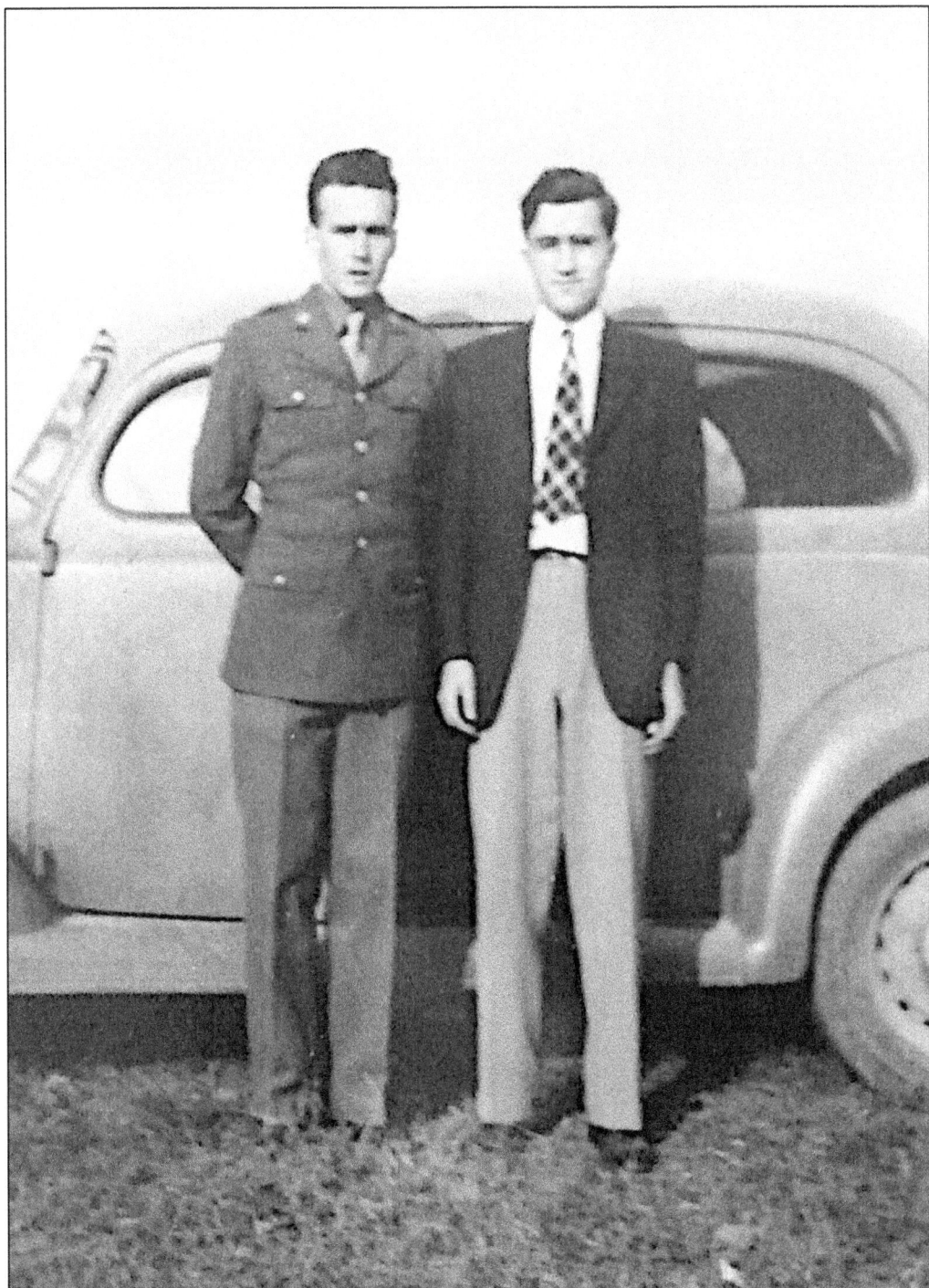

Ralph and Don, October 24, 1943

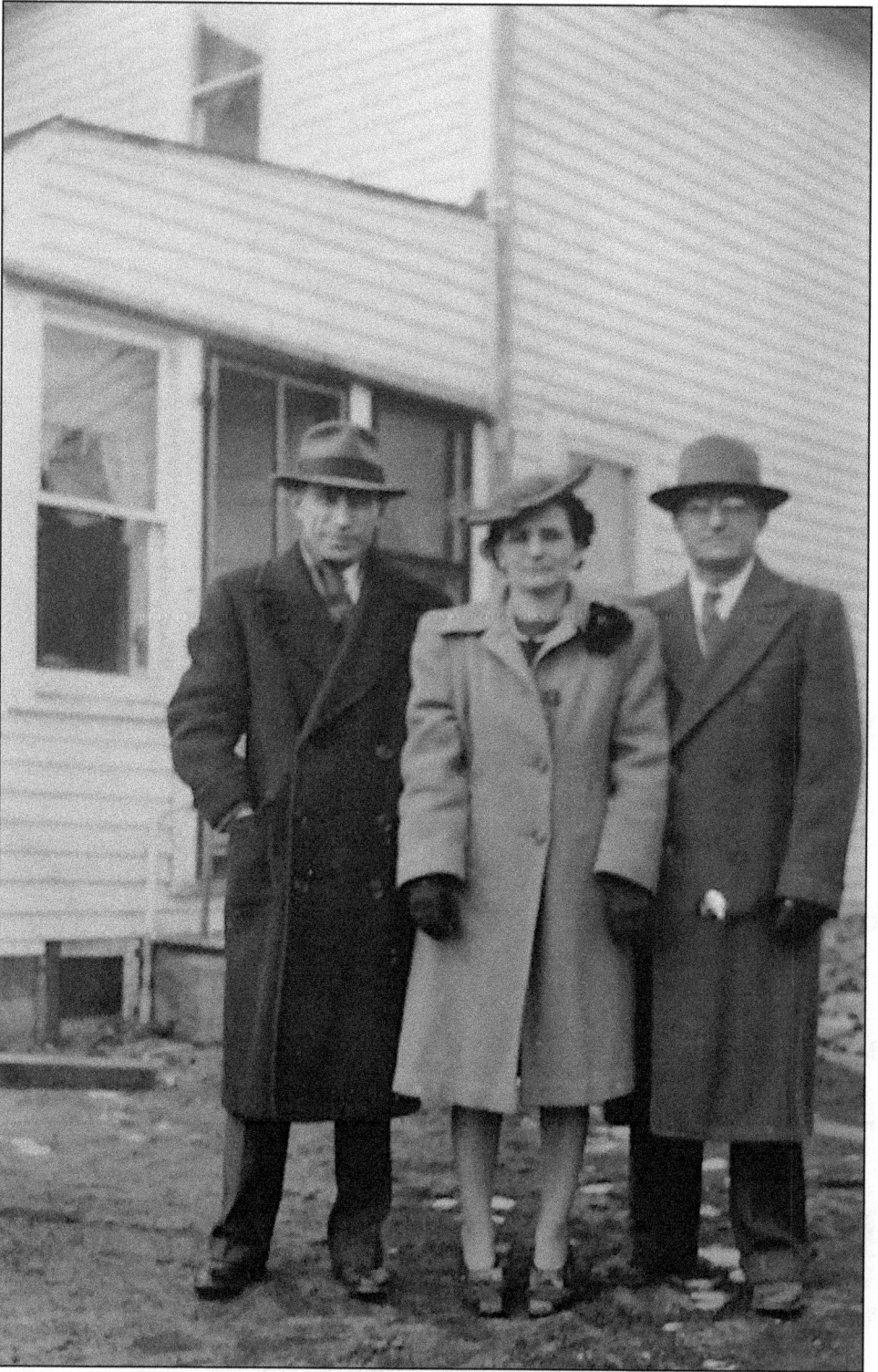

Dad's brother Frank, Mom, and Dad, March 12, 1944

Ralph at Camp Bowie, Texas, March 23, 1944

John and Marie's kids, October 9, 1944

Katie (Kathryn), Ralph, Gerry (Geraldine), Don (Donald),
Rusty (Lucille), Ray (Raymond)

Jerry (Gerald) Hackert, June 1944

Grandpa Ignatius Voigt and Grandma Mary Kraemer Schreder Voigt,
June 4, 1944

Grandma Mary, Ralph, and Mom
June 4, 1944

Family group at Pete Schreder home
June 4, 1944

Pete is second from the right with arms crossed. His son Richard is behind him wearing a baseball uniform.

Grandpa Voigt is the tallest one, near the middle in the back. You can see why they called him "Shorty." Grandma Mary Voigt is in front of him. Mom's sister Anna is next to Grandpa on his left.

Mom and Dad are in the back row, to Grandpa's right.

Grandma Mary, Ralph, Mom, and Dad
probably June 4, 1944

Gerry, Rusty, Ralph, and Katie
June 16, 1944

Ray, Ralph, and Don - John's three sons
June 16, 1944

John and Marie's family, 1944

Don, Gerry, Dad, Rusty, Mom, Katie, Ralph, Ray

Ralph and Jeannette Guck

Home in Bellingham, Minnesota from the top of the elevator
April 1942

In the foreground is the old elevator office roof, across the road from the elevator, in use in 1921 when my dad ran the elevator.

To the left of the house was a big garden that extended to the left to the end of the property. Note the line of trees at the left (east), and at the far end of the property (south). When we were little kids, we could climb one of the trees at the right end and swing from branch to branch like Tarzan, all the way to the gap at the corner where the gate was. Then we'd climb into the left-hand row of trees and swing again. What a playground that was!

To the left of the pump, at the end closest to the pump, were many kinds of rose bushes, then toward the back were currant bushes, and then a flower patch up to the entry gate.

Home by moonlight, Bellingham, April 19, 1943

Note the hand cart made by my dad John, used to deliver milk. To the left of the bicycle (Don and Ray's) is the cellar door to enter with the fresh milk to be cooled, filtered, and bottled in the cellar, and then delivered via the cart.

The right addition to the house, the upstairs with full windows around it, was used by the boys in the family for sleeping in spring, summer, and fall. Note the two chimneys, one for house heating in a dining room stove, and one to the right for the kitchen stove.

The upstairs right windowed room did not have the floor finished, so Grandpa Peter came and constructed a hardwood floor.

Behind the bicycle rear wheel was the top of the house cistern. This was soft water from rains collected off the roof and, if necessary, soft water delivered in a wooden tank drawn by horses from our neighbors on a farm to the south of us. The cistern fed to a pump and sink in the kitchen. The waste water fed to a cesspool to the south of the house.

The corner of the house and the attached entry could be enclosed with an old sheet and used as an outside place to bathe on hot summer days. (The tub in front was used for that.)

Home in Bellingham, from northwest driveway

Note the evergreen tree, left foreground, where my dad John, took pictures of the kids for First Communion, Confirmation, birthdays, and other special occasions. The pictures showed the tree from a sapling to its full-grown state, quite tall, as shown here.

To the right and behind the house, one can see the woodshed, and further back, the barn. The wash lines were to the right of the woodshed—no clothes dryers in those days.

Home in Bellingham, from the north

Note that the tree in front of the house is quite tall in the 1940s. When we arrived in 1932, it was quite little.

Home in Bellingham, from the northeast garden in the foreground

Note the chimney. It was inside the walls of the two bedrooms upstairs, and was for the kitchen stove below it and to heat those bedrooms in winter. The dining room also had a stove for heating the house and a register to heat the bedroom above for John and Marie.

Home in Bellingham, from the southwest

One summer, my mom decided I should trim the dead branches of these trees. I went up with ropes to keep safe. I was not going to be busy sawing and fall out of the tree and kill myself. It took a week or two to finish all the trimming. This photo is probably from 1944; note my car by the house. There was a low spot amongst the trees on the right where I could park the cars and get under them to change the oil.

All that area was lawn and we'd mow it with a push-mower, no engine! On the left side of the house was the ball field and the grass was very thick there. We kept it as a lawn. When we were growing up, on Sunday afternoons my dad John would bat flies out to us kids to catch and throw back. This area was also a great place to snare and trap gophers.

House at Bellingham from the southeast

December 31, 1944

This was the house that Dad's family lived in from 1932 to 1945. Ray's car is in front of the south side of the house. The windows that jutted out of the house behind the car opened into the parlor, where Mom always kept plants. There was a broad doorway to the left into the dining room.

Downstairs to the north, behind the parlor, was the kitchen. To the left, on the south side, was a window in the dining room. Above this was the window in Dad and Mom's bedroom, and behind that was the stairway. The window upstairs to the right, above the car, was the window in the girls' room; behind that was the boys' room; below it was the kitchen.

The addition on the right—the flat roof—had a bedroom upstairs, and the back entry was downstairs, with a kerosene stove for cooking and canning in summer. Upstairs in the addition was a bedroom that was entered from the boys' bedroom and had windows on three sides. When we first moved into the house, there was no floor in this bedroom, so Grandpa Peter came and installed it.

For heating in winter, we depended on the kitchen stove to also heat the boys' room above it, and a space heater in the dining room to heat Dad and Mom's bedroom above it. There were vents in the ceilings to help carry the heat upward.

Behind the car (unseen) was a cistern for soft water, filled with rainwater, and an occasional tank of soft water from the nearby Menzel farm. This was used in a sink-and-pump in the kitchen for wash-up and laundry; well water was used for all else. The sink emptied into a cesspool south of the house.

To the right of the house, one can see our pump—good water and the well never went dry. Beyond the well, one can see the east end of the elevator.

To the left of the house, one can see the entrance gate to the property on which Rusty would swing. The gate was generally open, but we closed it if the cows got out of their pastures.

Note the bicycle lying behind the car at the cellar door. Ray, when about 17, graduated from the bicycle to the car for getting around. In later years with the milk business, the cellar door entrance was very handy to reach the cool cellar for processing milk without tracking through the house.

Note the washtub over the front of the car; it was used for Saturday baths, for making sausage during butchering season, and for Monday laundry. Of course, we cleaned it thoroughly between these activities.

Barnyard of our place in Bellingham
December 31, 1944

Note the chicken house to the right. Mom got a separate chicken house for hundreds of chicks in spring. It was in the hayfield beyond the barn. Later, as the chicks were growing up, they were kept in the closed barn at night with cats to protect them from rats. The cows stayed in the pasture in summer.

Farmers Cooperative Elevator Company of Bellingham
December 31, 1944

Note the main elevator building, with a major addition of more grain bins in the closer view. Beyond the driveway entrance, my dad John managed a rebuild of a new pit, scales, and grain handling system to update the elevator. The milling operation to the right of the elevator entrance is the same even in 2017 as when we moved to Bellingham in 1932.

Gerry and Katie, Bellingham High School cheerleaders, 1945

Gerry and Mom on the porch in Bellingham

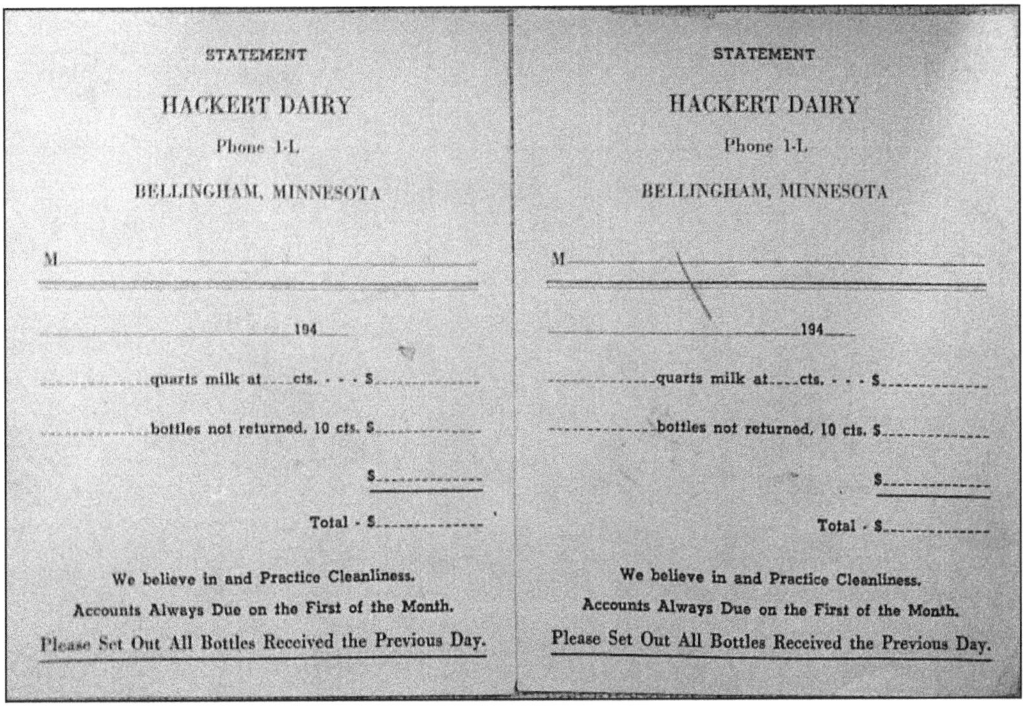

STATEMENT

HACKERT DAIRY

Phone 1-L

BELLINGHAM, MINNESOTA

M

194

quarts milk at cts. - - - $

bottles not returned, 10 cts. $

$

Total - $

We believe in and Practice Cleanliness.
Accounts Always Due on the First of the Month.
Please Set Out All Bottles Received the Previous Day.

Hackert Dairy order forms

Customers would leave an order form for bottled milk they needed. Milk delivery went on early in the morning, before school started, so the customers wouldn't be available in person to tell us what they wanted.

Moving out of Bellingham
March 24, 1945

In this photo, the truck is backed up to the front porch, the front door behind it. To move, we sold off the dairy business, all the pigs and chickens, and all the equipment at auction.

The window above the porch was Dad and Mom's bedroom. Just inside the front door was the stairway. The window on the left opened into the pantry off the kitchen.

Ray, 1945

My high school graduation picture—I hadn't known we needed to dress up, so I had to borrow a tie from Dean and a jacket from Charlie, my classmates, for this picture.

Dad's older brother, Frank and Frank's oldest son, Jerry (Gerald)

John and Marie's family

Front: Rusty (Lucille), Dad, Mom, Katie (Kathryn)

Back: Gerry (Geraldine), Ralph, Don (Donald), Ray (Raymond)

My college classmates, May 1946

Ray, Roy, my brother Ralph, Jose, my brother Don, and Bob

We attended St. John's University together.

Ray, 1949

My college graduation picture

Hackert's Grocery, St. Cloud, 1945

The storefront faces 9th Avenue S, and to the right is 10th Street S. The store has a full basement for storage of the supplies for sale.

Home in St. Cloud, 226 10 St. S
Easter 1945

Note the porch behind the car on the right with steps up to it and an entrance into the kitchen. The doorway beyond the car on the left, Ray's car, leads to steps down from the kitchen, and continues to the basement. To the right of the house, one can see the car shed.

Dad and Mom, February 1946

Edwin and Theresa Linn Hackert

Edwin and Theresa lived nearby in Bellingham. He ran the Peavey Elevator while my dad John ran the Farmers Elevator in Bellingham. Many evenings they would talk about the elevator business. Later they moved to Brush, Colorado. They had only one daughter, Margaret, who died when she was 20, so they have no descendants. Edwin was the youngest son of Grandpa Peter Sr.

Mom and Dad

Anamoose, North Dakota
April 1, 1947, the old house

We visited this old house again in 1947. No one was living there, so we looked around the property inside and out. We kids who were born in North Dakota were the ones who went on this trip (except Don – he was working).

The road in front of the house ended to the left. Note the front screen porch, where my dad John often took pictures of the kids, particularly of the littlest ones. To the right of the porch was an extension, a room which had sliding doors leading to the living room. The extension was where the tree at Christmas stood.

To the right beyond the house was the car shed. There was a barn behind the house for our family cow and chickens. Our garden fronted on the end of the road to the left.

The House in North Dakota

Note the right side of the front of the house, which was a doorway into the living room.

My mother Marie and my dad John

My dad John and mother Marie

June 21, 1981

Dad and Mom's 60th wedding anniversary

My last picture with Dad, 1986

Ralph, my dad John, Ray

Oldest elevator building still operating at Farmers Cooperative
Elevator Company of Bellingham, November 16, 2017

This elevator building is still about the same as in 1945, with the scale, grain handling equipment, the milling part, and the office. Little has noticeably changed. Ray is in front of the driveway into the elevator.

4—772.

The United States of America,

TO ALL TO WHOM THESE PRESENTS SHALL COME, GREETING:

Homestead Certificate No. 7682

Application 120121

Whereas there has been deposited in the GENERAL LAND OFFICE of the United States a CERTIFICATE of the Register of the Land Office at *Marshall Minnesota*, whereby it appears that, pursuant to the Act of Congress approved 20th May, 1862. "To secure Homesteads to actual settlers on the public domain." and the acts supplemental thereto, the claim of *Peter H Hackert* has been established and duly consummated in conformity to law for the *West half of the North East quarter and the East half of the North West quarter of section fourteen in Township one hundred and nineteen North of Range forty-six West of the Fifth Principal meridian in Minnesota containing one hundred and sixty acres*

according to the Official Plat of the Survey of the said Land returned to the GENERAL LAND OFFICE by the SURVEYOR GENERAL.

Now know ye, That there is therefore granted by the UNITED STATES unto the said *Peter H Hackert* the tract of Land above described: TO HAVE AND TO HOLD the said tract of Land, with the appurtenances thereof, unto the said *Peter H Hackert* and to his heirs and assigns forever.

In testimony whereof I, *William McKinley* President of the United States of America, have caused these letters to be made Patent, and the Seal of the General Land Office to be hereunto affixed.

Given under my hand, at the City of Washington, the *Eighteenth* day of *August*, in the year of Our Lord one thousand eight hundred and *Ninety seven*, and of the Independence of the United States the one hundred and *twenty second*.

[L. S.]

By the President: *William McKinley*

By *J M McKean* Sec'y.

C H Bruch Recorder of the General Land Office.

Register of Grandpa Peter's homesteaded land

First House?

As best we, Geraldine and Ray, know, this is the house that was on the Peter Hackert homestead when Grandpa Peter first lived there. This building was used for storage on the farm as late as the 1930s. My dad John was probably born there.

❖ *Index* ❖

John Hackert Building 6, 133

www.ingramcontent.com/pod-product-compliance
Lightning Source LLC
Chambersburg PA
CBHW080541090426
42734CB00016B/3176

9 781628 063523